Learning to Love Yourself Despite Being Unloved, Feeling Self-Hatred, and Having Self-Loathing

Jennifer Butler Green

Contents

Are you happy with your life right now? What would make you happy? Do you have a plan for getting it? Would you like some help? I might be able to help you. Are you interested? Sign up for my newsletter. I give out a free workbook to help with social anxiety issues so those who sign up. I also give out limited copies of audiobook versions of my books. I also write more books and posting articles that can help deal with other issues related to social anxiety. There's a community that I'm building for people who are going through similar issues as you. If it's okay with you, I'd also like to get your feedback so I can write more about things that could help you. Does that sound like something that might interest you? I hope it does, because I need your help in helping others too. I have been in your shoes before, so I know how it feels. Join my newsletter and let's all help each other. Does that sound good? Visit my website now! The link is below and signup for my newsletter!

http://jen.green

I. Introduction

The working title for this book was supposed to be "How to Love Yourself: A Psychological Approach," but then I remembered how back when I was younger, I hated how people would tell me that I should learn to love myself. It was like these people are asking me to do the impossible. How can I love myself when I don't even know how to begin? Am I supposed to just tell myself "I love me" and everything will be alright?

I want to help you learn to love yourself but at the same time, I want you to learn to love yourself in a way that isn't judgmental. I understand that loving yourself is not easy especially for someone who has spent years loathing themselves. I have read some books on how to love yourself and it's almost always about telling yourself that you love yourself and I think it's oversimplifying things.

You got this book because you feel like there is a void you have to fill, and you believe that learning how to love yourself will fill that void. The good news is that this void, the sense of emptiness you feel is something that can definitely be filled.

Loving yourself means having good health, having healthy relationships and being truly happy inside and out. I want to teach you how to love yourself, without being a narcissist or becoming a selfish person who only thinks about yourself. While it can be said that true self-love is internal – meaning that it shouldn't be affected by what's outside yourself(e.g. your social life), I would like to add that while true self-love begins inside you, it should still take into consideration what is outside you and how it affects the people around you and the relationships you have.

What I want to teach you to understand yourself on a deeper level, knowing your strengths and weaknesses for you to make the best possible decisions and to set realistic goals and be able to achieve them. I want you to be able to achieve true happiness, not the shallow pleasures that don't last. During the course of this book I might use the phrases "lack of self-love," "not having enough love for yourself," "self-loathing," or "not loving yourself" interchangeably.

Are you worthy of being loved?

The lack of self-love usually stems from the feeling of unworthiness that a person feels. You think you're too ugly to be loved. You think you've made some horrible mistakes that cannot be forgiven. You think that because of certain things in your life or things about your family you don't deserve to be respected. Because of this feeling of unworthiness, you don't value yourself and you don't think that other people will like you. It's painful. It eats you inside. You can't sleep. You keep worrying. You can't relax. You feel like there's something wrong with you that you need to fix.

Are you letting others walk all over you?

Because you feel unworthy of being loved, because you think that nobody will ever love you, because you don't value yourself, you look to other people to give you the love that you so badly crave. You give other people everything you have. Even if you're already deep in debt you still buy the most expensive gifts you can get for your friends' birthdays. You're injured or sick but you still make an effort to help a friend move into her new apartment. Some of your friends like to invite you to go out because whenever you go out you pay for their food and drinks. You do your friends a lot of favors and you don't mind at all because they're the only friends you have and nobody else would want to be friends with someone like you.

Are you living in the past?

You're not happy with the way your life is going. You want to be loved and respected for who you are but you're not sure about yourself. How can you expect to be loved after all that has happened? After what you have done how can you expect to be respected by other people? You screwed up. You made a fool of yourself. People laughed at you. People got hurt because of you. Your family is ashamed of you. How can you forgive yourself? How can you stop the painful memories from playing over and over in your head?

Are you having difficulty trusting yourself and other people?

You have trouble trusting yourself. You second-guess every decision you make. You can't rely on your memories because you might have been remembering things differently. You always have to check and double-check everything. You find it hard to trust other people. You're afraid to call in a plumber to fix the leak in your sink because you're worried that they might steal something or cheat you into getting more things fixed and end up paying too much. The store is crowded, and you feel like people are observing you and talking about you. You pick the wrong item but because you're afraid that the people who have seen you might think you're stupid if you put it back so you go ahead and buy the thing anyway.

Are you having trouble maintaining lasting relationships?

You feel unworthy of being loved. You have a hole inside of you so deep that you're expecting someone else to fill the hole. You have the friends that you go all the way for because you don't believe that you can ever make new friends. You have recurring painful memories from past screw-ups and so you're scared of ever screwing up and worse, you get upset over every little mistake. Because you expect your partner to fill the hole and because you don't think that you deserve to be loved, you feel like your partner isn't giving you enough. You have trouble trusting your partner because you're afraid that they will eventually leave you. You get upset over the little things and you expect too much and nothing that your partner can give you is ever enough.

Does any of that sound familiar to you? Have you ever had these thoughts in your head? Have you ever experienced being in that situation? Those are just some of the things that bother you when you don't love yourself. You've probably heard of the saying that in order to love others you must first love yourself. I personally believe that this is true. If you don't know how to love yourself, you will try to get others to love you but it will never be enough no matter what you do simply because you really don't know what love is – how could you when you can't even love yourself?

Don't worry, I'm not here to judge you. I understand and that's not because I'm a psychologist who has studied how people think and behave. I know because I have at one point in my life did not love myself. I know because I have been around people who don't love themselves. It's hard when nobody loves you, but it's even harder if you don't even love yourself.

By the end of this book, I'm hoping to have taught you enough that you're able to show yourself a little love and respect. For now, let's discuss the signs that tell you that you may be lacking some much-needed self-love.

II. The Signs That You Lack of Self-Love

Before I start teaching you about how to love yourself, I think it's important first to identify the signs and symptoms of lacking self-love. Try to see if you have any of these signs or have anything similar. Keep these signs you have in mind because you need to be able to identify specific symptoms to understand your problem and develop a more effective solution that fits your particular needs.

1. You're Too Focused on Productivity and Feel Guilty About Taking a Break or Having Fun

Wanting to be more productive is a good thing. You want to be able to do more work and accomplish more of your tasks and goals that you set, however, if you're too into your work and don't think that you deserve a break or if having fun is no longer a part of your process, then perhaps it's time to take a step back and re-evaluate.

As they say, too much of a good thing can be bad and taking a break and having fun is definitely something that should be done on occasion. It's okay to prioritize work and productivity especially when you have a deadline or a pile of work needing to be finished and when you're still okay with taking a break when you get tired or overwhelmed.

It's a problem when you start thinking that you don't deserve to take a break or when you actually take a break and have fun only to feel guilty about it later. You keep pushing yourself to the limit and you feel that taking even a short break is a waste of your precious time. You work yourself to death because you believe that taking time to have fun or spend time with your loved ones keeps you away from becoming successful.

Loving yourself means also making yourself happy and if you're not doing things that make you happy then it means you don't love yourself enough.

2. You Believe that You're Stuck with Current Situation and You No Longer Have Any Dreams and Aspirations

Have you completely given up on your dreams? Have you completely given up on making things better? Some people just develop so much self-doubt that they no longer believe that they can ever achieve anything meaningful.

Without having dreams of better things or aspiring to something greater than your current situation, you are completely wasting your potential. It's one thing to feel contentment where you feel that you've already achieved everything you can, and it's another thing to feel that you can't achieve anything and completely give up on trying.

You probably still have dreams of a better life or improving your situation but you're no longer doing anything to reach those dreams or improve your situation because you've accepted that this is your lot in life. You let this limiting belief take you over and your life has become stagnant.

You stop believing in your own potential and you let yourself settle for mediocrity. You feel like it's futile to even try because you're sure that trying will only result in failure. You hate your current situation but you're scared to make changes because you're afraid that you'll only make things worse.

3. You Keep Comparing Yourself to Others and are Extremely Self-Critical

Everyone is unique. Each of us has a unique set of circumstances, personalities, talents, and abilities. Some people are simply better than others in some things and that's just a fact of life. It's okay to feel a little envious over what other people have that we don't and it's okay to have people whom we think are better than us. It's also okay to be a little self-critical especially when we screw up and it's okay to be a little insecure about some small part of ourselves. That's really just the way things are.

Sometimes we can't help but compare ourselves with other people. It's what makes the advertising industry lucrative. We see a beautiful actress using an anti-aging cream and we want to look young and beautiful like this actress, so we buy the product. Men want to look as big and strong as the athletes featured on supplement labels so they buy the supplements hoping to get the same results. We naturally compare ourselves to other people, especially the ones who we think are doing better than us.

The problem is when comparing yourself to someone else becomes excessive to the point of obsession and you can't seem to stop doing it. It's a problem when you start seeing yourself as ultimately inferior to other people and you start punishing yourself for making small mistakes and when you feel like you're not as good as someone else.

You get frustrated and start loathing yourself for not having what other people have or not getting the same results as others. You blame yourself for everything that goes wrong even if it's something that's beyond your control. You consider yourself a failure because you're not as successful as someone you know.

4. You Hate the Way You Look

Related to the previous entry, this is when you can't accept something about your physical attributes. While feeling a little insecure about some part of your body and features is normal, it becomes a problem when you let the insecurity consume you and you become overly self-critical of your physical features and punish yourself.

This punishment can come in the form or giving up on trying to look good. You stop fixing your hair, you stop caring about what clothes to wear, you stop grooming yourself and you stop caring about eating healthy and getting regular exercise. Sometimes the punishment takes on the exact opposite. You become extremely obsessed with looking perfect that you spend all your money on fancy things, even going as far as getting plastic surgery because you want to look perfect.

Eventually, you develop a host of issues like eating disorders and body dysmorphia because of your obsession with your physical appearance. No amount of makeup, clothes, or body modifications is enough to make you feel beautiful. You crave for perfection that you will never realistically achieve and you go to extraordinary lengths, even taking huge risks just to look perfect.

5. You Have Extremely High-Risk Tendencies

It's okay to take occasional, calculated risks if you stand to gain something. However, it's different when you are actively making choices that you already know you'll regret later or taking an unnecessarily high amount of risk. It's an even more dangerous sign when you deliberately put yourself in harm's way for cheap thrills.

This reminds me of a good friend back in college who had gambling problems and a generally high-risk tendency. He once had to borrow money from me and other friends because he lost his entire month's budget gambling in an underground casino.

He also participates in underground races and does a lot of base jumping. We used to do interventions, but he never takes us seriously. He keeps saying that he doesn't really feel alive and these things that he does is his way to feel alive. He just went away one day and none of us heard from him again. I sincerely hope that he's doing okay.

As I said, it's normal to take risks but it's only good if you have taken the time to really think about it and you're not unnecessarily risking your life or property. I believe that in order to succeed in life, a person needs to take certain risks but these risks should be manageable calculated risks.

When you find yourself betting too much for a relatively small amount of gain or if you stop caring whether you lose a lot just for the thrill of taking a risk then you have a problem. People who don't love themselves don't care about what they are putting on the line and risk everything for small, irrational potential gains.

6. You Have Self-Destructive Behaviors

Do you have any behaviors that cause you harm? Anything that gives you short-term pleasure at the cost of harming yourself or the people you care about may be considered self-destructive behaviors. Just the fact that you are deliberately harming yourself means that you don't love yourself enough. You're supposed to take care of yourself but instead, you hurt yourself. You settle for a relatively small and short-term relief even if you already know that it's not going to be good for you in the long run.

You keep smoking even if you already know that you risk getting lung cancer. You drink excessively and sometimes use it as an excuse for bad behavior. You do a lot of drugs and take large doses in an attempt to maximize the pleasure you'll feel even if you could die from an overdose. You practice unsafe, unprotected sex with prostitutes or partners with questionable backgrounds.

It could also be that maybe you're not aware that you're sabotaging yourself or simply don't notice the damage you're doing because you don't take time to consider your actions and what the consequences are for such actions. The worst thing is when you don't even listen to the people who care about you anymore and you think that they're just holding you back. You stopped thinking of consequences and just go for whatever feels good at the time.

7. You're Too Needy

Everyone craves attention one way or another. We each have the desire to be appreciated and we all need to be needed. It's just how we all are. We're social creatures that need affirmation and appreciation from others. That's why we all try to express ourselves in interesting ways like showing off our talents or augmenting our features with makeup and fashion.

The problem is when the attention-seeking makes you too clingy or overbearing. When you constantly feel the need affirmation and the approval of other people and go to great lengths to get the attention you seek, it tends to drive people away instead of drawing them closer.

Sometimes, you give away so much of yourself just to gain the approval of others. You have such a low opinion of your worth that you no longer have standards and just go for anything that seems to be within reach especially when it comes to your relationships. Another way this happens is when you put too much value on others that you put them on a pedestal and worship them. You feel a strong need to earn their approval that you're willing to do just about anything for them, even if it causes you harm.

You get serious in your relationships too quickly and you feel the need to lock the other person in right away. You feel the need to be with them every minute and you call or text them excessively and when they don't answer you immediately you freak out. You keep checking your phone for a reply and you tend to imagine a lot of worst-case scenarios on why they aren't answering you without even taking into consideration the fact that they might be busy with something.

8. You're Too Afraid to Make Mistakes

Like I said earlier, it's okay to make the occasional mistake. You're only human after all, and there are things that you miss or overlook. Being afraid of making a mistake is also natural, I mean who likes screwing up right? When you find yourself continually overthinking every little thing and get paralysis by analysis, then it's time to consider that you may have a problem.

You're so scared of being ridiculed that you don't share your opinions even when asked about it. You go along with whatever other people tell you to do, and you don't complain even if you're suffering because you're afraid that doing your own thing is an even bigger mistake. You let other people choose for you all the time, ranging from the simplest thing like picking ice cream flavors to major ones like picking a car model.

When you actually make decisions, you can't help but second-guess and wonder if you can still take it back. Whenever you're faced with a choice, you try to analyze every detail and you try to predict everything that could go wrong until you end up having to unnecessarily delay or try to get someone else to make a choice for you.

You're afraid of taking responsibility for any negative consequences of your choices that you make everything into a democratic process where you ask for everyone's opinions and go with whatever choice has more votes, even if inside your head, you know that it's not the best course of action.

9. You Have Poor Communication Skills

A little shyness and awkwardness is okay but when you're having a real struggle in approaching and talking to other people then you might want to re-evaluate yourself. It's okay to feel a little embarrassed when trying to approach someone, but it should never be to a point where you're unable to relay something important because you're too afraid to talk to people.

When you know that you have to approach someone and speak up but physically are unable to or start feeling really anxious about just expressing yourself even a little bit then it's a problem. It's a real sign of trouble when you're having trouble expressing yourself that you keep feeling that you're not being heard or understood.

You know you have to talk to someone about something important, but you agonize over how to best approach them and how to word it correctly only to end up saying it in the worst possible time and in the worst possible way because you got too nervous about it. When faced with having to tell someone something negative, you pick the least personal method like sending an email or texting because you're too afraid of facing the other person.

You tend to speak too much without thinking about what comes out of your mouth and you fail to listen. Worse, you misinterpret a lot of things because you tend to overthink and try to find hidden meanings even with the simplest of statements.

10. You're a Perfectionist

When you expect everything to be perfect, then you're just setting yourself up for disappointment. You expect everything to go your way so you go to extreme lengths to make it happen just the way you planned. You expect other people to behave the way you want them to and you get extremely upset when they don't.

You get the best in fashion because you want to keep this image of being cool or being classy. You get all the cool new gadgets also in an effort to look cool and you consciously act in a certain way in order to get approval and praise, but then you get upset when you don't get the perfect feedback that you crave.

You have a strong tendency to plan everything down to the smallest of details in an attempt to control things and people and you get extremely upset if something doesn't go as planned even if the desired end result is achieved.

You expect nothing less than perfect from yourself and the people around you that you always end up being disappointed. It's just not healthy to expect everything to be perfect, you're essentially setting yourself up to feel disappointed and frustrated all the time.

11. You're Too Afraid of Upsetting Other People that You've Become a People-Pleaser

What normal healthy person enjoys upsetting other people right? Nothing wrong with avoiding unnecessary conflict but if you find yourself constantly giving in to what other people want even

if it's not something that you like then you may have a problem.

You keep feeling used because well, you let other people keep using you because you're too afraid that they won't like you anymore if you don't give them what they want from you. You're afraid to express your opinion whenever it's against someone else's and you tend to just outwardly agree to everything they say. You always take the side of whomever you are with at the moment and change your views and opinions to fit whatever you feel that they need to hear at the time.

You laugh the hardest even at the unfunniest of jokes and you give the most expensive gifts even if it puts you deep in debt because you want to be the "bestest best friend ever." You make yourself available anytime, all the time for your friends that you're willing to call in sick from work or even quit if need be just to be there when your friend "needs someone right now."

When you find yourself having a hard time telling people "no" or when you just go along with whatever other people want even if it greatly inconveniences you and especially when it gets to the point where doing things for others even if it hurts you then you have a serious self-love issue that definitely needs to be addressed.

12. You Assume the Worst and Expect to Fail

Whenever you do something you find yourself bracing for impact because you assume that something is going to go wrong and everything will come crashing down in flames. While you're not really struggling with choices and decision-making and you don't have trouble acting on your decisions, you find yourself in a constant state of hyper-alertness because you believe that something is bound to go wrong and disaster is going to strike any minute soon.

You worry about what you might have said wrong when a date has not replied to your texts right away. You try to play everything back in your head to see where you screwed up and you end up wasting time and energy thinking about the many ways you might

have done things wrong and it's stressing you out.
When you actually manage to be in a relationship,
they don't last long because you drive the other
person away just when things start to get better.
You're suspicious about every little thing because
you're scared that they'll just end up leaving you
anyway.

You never give anything your all because in your
head you believe that anything you try is futile. You
don't trust in words of encouragement because you
don't want to believe that you can be successful, and
you don't want to get your hopes up.

13. You Feel Unworthy of Anything Good

Someone praises you and you deny the praise
because you don't believe that you've done enough.
You reject anyone who tries to get close to you
because you believe that you're not good enough to
be worthy of connections. You feel the need to

apologize for every little thing even if it's not even your fault. You're stuck in the past, reliving your mistakes over and over and are unable to forgive yourself.

Whenever something good actually happens to you, you immediately get overcome by dread because you think that there's a price to pay for your good fortune. Whenever someone tries to be nice to you, you think that they're after something. You don't accept help because you're afraid to owe anyone favors.

This I believe is the most dangerous of all the signs and symptoms because it greatly affects your quality of life. You have given up on achieving anything good and when something good actually happens you don't feel that you deserve it. If you feel unworthy then everything in your life becomes a source of pain.

III. What Do You Need in Order to Love Yourself?

Self-love is composed of a few factors and related concepts and before I can tell you what I mean about loving yourself the right way, I believe that these concepts must be explained. While different sources count different components, I personally believe that it comes down to several main components which are having a healthy level of self-esteem, self-confidence, self-acceptance, self-awareness, self-respect, and personal empowerment.

At first glance each of these components may look similar and, in a way, they are. However, there are also a few significant differences that you need to be aware of in order to understand each component and how each of them affects how you love yourself.

All of these factors combined make up what I believe to be self-love and if you want to learn to love yourself, you would need to learn and develop each of these components to healthy levels. Since my aim in this book is to try to teach you how to love yourself correctly, I want you to understand what you need to have in order to be able to completely love yourself.

1. Self-Esteem

In the simplest of terms, self-esteem is generally what you think of yourself. It can be said that confident people have a high degree of self-esteem while those lacking in confidence have low self-esteem. It usually develops through a combination of upbringing and personal experiences that shapes the way we view ourselves.

Most kids who grow up with loving parents initially develop a high level of self-esteem because parents would always tend to compliment their child regardless of their actual abilities. It's the same with society in general. Normal adults always praise children and are generally encouraging. No reasonable person would think to give a child negative criticism.

As a result, we as children have a high-level of self-esteem because most of the feedback we get is positive and adults try to be as kind to us as they can. As we grow up, the feedback we are given becomes more honest and our view of ourselves start to shift into a more realistic one.

Self-Esteem is dynamic. It changes depending on a person's status and perception of themselves. During times of failure, self-esteem normally goes down because we generally also receive negative feedback while in periods of success, self-esteem goes up because the feedback we get is also positive. It's your evaluation of yourself, based on the feedback you get.

It's not always grounded in reality, and it can be subject to changes in a person's condition or social environment. It's also a result of the accumulation of the experiences and affirmations that we have had since childhood which builds an image in our minds about who and what we are and where we ideally should stand in the social order.

2. Self-confidence

Self-confidence generally refers to your faith in your abilities. It develops from awareness or at least a perception of what you're capable of. For example, if you believe that you're terrible at math, then your confidence in tackling mathematical problems will naturally be low. If you think that you're a terrible dancer, then you would tend to avoid dancing-related activities.

Like I said earlier, it's about your faith in your abilities and is not always tied to reality. You can be confident about your singing abilities because you believe that you have a golden voice while in reality other people who hear you sing think the opposite. Because of your misguided confidence in your singing abilities, you might be inclined to actively promote yourself as a singer regardless of what your actual voice quality really is.

If you ever watch talent shows on TV, you'll see a lot of people who have a high level of confidence in their abilities. They view themselves as extremely talented and try to impress the judges and audience only to be disappointed when they do not win or even get angry if they receive a fair criticism from the judges.

It's because self-confidence does not necessarily reflect your actual abilities but instead reflects what you think of your abilities. It's similar to self-esteem in that it usually comes from your upbringing and personal experiences, but it differs from it by being more specific. You usually develop your confidence in particular abilities because of the feedback you have received whenever you display these abilities.

When I was little, I used to like singing in public. I used to sing at school presentations and I really thought I had a great voice because my parents would always compliment me whenever I sang. During school presentations, the audience would clap after I sing and of course they did, what kind of adult would tell a child that their voice was terrible? This made me confident about my singing abilities.

When I grew up and started hanging out with people other than my parents, I started getting feedback that wasn't always positive whenever I sing.

Unfortunately, people become more honest in their feedback when you're no longer a child so I lost confidence in my singing. While I still love to sing, I'm no longer that confident about it that I would never sing on stage with an audience unless I was really forced to do it.

On the other hand, I feel confident about my writing skills. While I do admit that I'm not at a Pulitzer-prize winning level, I'm confident enough that I decided to try my hand and writing books and as described earlier, my confidence in writing can change as I get feedback on my books.

3. Self-Acceptance

Self-Acceptance, on the other hand, is when you learn to accept yourself for what you are. It's when you forgive yourself for all your faults and failures. It's when you appreciate your individuality regardless of how others perceive you. It's close to self-love as having self-acceptance means recognizing your flaws and knowing all your negative traits but still appreciate yourself.

Unlike self-esteem and self-confidence which are generally affected by other people's feedback, self-acceptance is something you attain despite the feedback you get. It's internal and more of a conscious choice rather than something that easily changes depending on what other people think.

When you learn to accept yourself, you don't judge yourself, and you don't compare yourself to others. It's being aware that you have specific weaknesses, but you don't let the awareness of these weaknesses bring down your opinion of yourself.

It's accepting your limitations as a human being. It's recognizing that you are not perfect, you make mistakes and you're not good at everything but still be okay with it. In other words, it's being content with yourself.

4. Self-Awareness

Self-awareness is similar to self-acceptance in the sense that it's the acknowledgment of your traits. It's about recognizing the changes in your emotions as they happen and exerting a degree of control of your actions following these emotional changes. It's understanding how these emotions affect your thought processes and knowing how you act in response to these emotions.

Having self-awareness is also similar to self-acceptance in that it's also about having an accurate assessment of your own weaknesses and limitations, but unlike self-acceptance, it's more about knowing. how these weaknesses and limitations affect the world around you. Basically, it's about knowing how to control your own behavior despite your emotions instead of letting your emotions control how you behave.

It's like the idea of professionalism. You act according to how you're supposed to in order to get the job done correctly, regardless of how you feel about your boss or your coworkers. You treat your boss and your coworkers with respect despite feeling intense dislike for them because you understand that you need to cooperate with them in order to get the job done.

Having self-awareness means understanding that your emotional state can affect your performance and behavior. It's knowing how to interact with your environment and other people in a morally-acceptable manner despite your emotional state. Having self-awareness means that you know how to control yourself.

5. Self-Respect

In simple terms, having self-respect means having pride in yourself and as a result, you behave in such a way that upholds your sense of honor and dignity. It's sometimes easy to confuse having a high degree of self-esteem or confidence with a high level of self-respect, but unlike self-esteem, having self-respect does not mean simply having a high opinion of yourself.

It's knowing what you're worth. It's having reasonable standards for yourself and behaving according to those standards. You don't settle for less because you know how much your worth and you don't hesitate to ask for what you deserve.

You're probably familiar with the phrase "Don't sink to their level" right? Having self-respect means exactly that. It means not compromising your own standards for anyone, even if they don't have any standards. It's about valuing yourself and because you value yourself, you don't let other people treat you any less no matter who they are.

Having self-respect also means that you have integrity. Your standards apply regardless of the situation. You don't bend your own rules or lower your standards just because it's easier to do so in certain situations.

If you have self-respect, you don't feel the need to beg for anyone's approval because for you, just knowing your own worth is all the approval you need. Basically, self-respect combines the elements of self-esteem, self-acceptance, and self-awareness in that you have a reasonable opinion of yourself, you're aware of your weaknesses and limitations, and you keep your actions within an acceptable moral standard.

It means knowing who and what you are and taking responsibility for your actions. It means that you feel worthy of being loved and accepted by others. It's acting with honor and dignity because you know that you deserve to be treated with respect.

It also means knowing how to properly ask for what you deserve and standing up for yourself if you're not treated with respect. You don't allow other people to give you less than what you ask for and you don't let other people disrespect you.

As a result, having self-respect means you also treat others with the same level of respect because you know that treating other people poorly demeans you. Having self-respect also tends to make other people treat you with respect because they see that you have standards and that you behave according to your own standards.

6. Personal Empowerment

Personal empowerment is taking control of your life in a positive way. It's taking all the above factors in order to determine your own worth and then using everything you know about yourself to set realistic goals and using your abilities to achieve them. It's knowing your weaknesses and aiming to improve on them and it's knowing your strengths and using them to advance yourself.

Having personal empowerment means knowing how to take control of your circumstances in order to achieve your personal goals. It's also about understanding your own strengths and weaknesses well, making you better equipped in dealing with any problems that you encounter. You know how to recognize opportunities and know how to take advantage of them appropriately in order to succeed.

It doesn't simply mean having the power to make things happen. It also means knowing how to set realistic goals and having the freedom and the ability to make conscious decisions and taking the appropriate actions in order to achieve these goals.

IV. Your Personality and its Role in Developing Self-Love

Given the factors above, loving yourself seems to be about developing a healthy personality. Before we are to discuss how to develop a healthy personality, it's important to first identify the things that we lack or the problems we have that keep us from developing our personality. We will discuss a few theories about how personality develops and how certain imbalances, inadequacies or situations negatively impact the development of a healthy personality.

Psychoanalytic Theory

The father of psychology Sigmund Freud founded what is now known as Psychoanalytic Theory, which became the foundation of many modern principles we psychologists' study and use today. In it, he teaches that personality has 3 parts: The Id, Superego, and the Ego.

The Id is basically the selfish part of us. It's the part of us that creates our desires, the part that only wants what feels good and it wants it immediately. Do you remember those drawings or tv shows where they show a person having an angel on one ear and a devil on the other? The Id is basically devil who only tells you what you want to hear, the one who tells you that if you want it you should just go for it. It should be noted however that unlike the devil who wants to get you in trouble, the Id is simply all about pleasure with no motives of its own.

The Superego, on the other hand, is the part of us that's idealistic, the one that is concerned with morality – basically what we call the "conscience," the part that wants to keep us good and honest and the one that wants us to play by the rules. It would be the angel on the other ear telling you what is right and appropriate and reminds you not to do the wrong thing.

The Ego is the part that looks at the choices and makes decisions. It's also the one that faces the consequences of these choices and decisions. Basically, it's the person and it operates on the idea that while the Id has to be satisfied, the concerns of the superego also have to be taken into consideration. It balances our thoughts and actions in such a way that we would gain pleasure while at the same time doing it in a realistic and socially acceptable manner.

According to this theory, when people dislike or even hate themselves, it's usually the result or a byproduct of something that messes up this arrangement. Sometimes the Ego miscalculates and gives priority to the Id, suffers from a heavy backlash, and subsequently lets the superego take the lead from that point onwards. While the superego is what tells you what is socially and morally acceptable, it is definitely not always good for you.

Additionally, Freud also places much emphasis on the role of sex in the development of personality in his Psychosexual Development theory. He proposes that personality is developed mostly from an early age as a person goes through specific stages of development. These stages in order of progression are Oral, Anal, Phallic, Latency, and Genital. In these stages, satisfaction is focused on specific areas and any lack of the required type of satisfaction during these stages creates a fixation. These fixations result in an adult having behaviors that are characteristic of the particular stage where the fixation originated.

The oral stage starts from birth and lasts until the first year of life. In this stage, the libido is centered in the mouth. This means that most of a person's satisfaction is derived from putting things in the mouth such as feeding, sucking and biting. Adults with a fixation on this stage are supposed to become nail-biters or have other behaviors that involve putting things in their mouth.

The anal stage follows right after and goes on until the third year of life and this time, the libido centers around the anus and satisfaction is derived from defecating. He puts much emphasis on potty training, stating that the way you were potty trained results in certain behaviors like how you approach cleanliness and how you react to authority.

The Phallic stage follows and lasts up to six years old. This stage is a little controversial, so I'll just explain it as the stage where gender identities are developed and where the concept of masturbation arises.

The latency follows the Phallic stage and lasts until the end of puberty. During this stage, the libido is mostly dormant, and the individual is more focused on developing new skills and acquiring knowledge.

The genital stage is the final stage that lasts through adulthood. The libido is directed towards sexual intercourse with the opposite sex. This is where sexual experimentation happens, and intimate relationships develop. Fixations during this stage result in sexual perversion.

The psychosexual development theory is highly controversial and has many opponents, but it is important to note here for our purposes that Freud's theory emphasizes that that cause of certain behaviors originates from the needs that we have from an early age, including whether these needs are met or not, and how these needs are met. In simple terms, how we are today is the result of our childhood.

Trait Theory

Trait theory began from the work of early American psychologist Gordon Allport. Unlike Freud's psychoanalytic theory that uses a one-size-fits-all approach in that it tries to be the theory that explains the behaviors of all humanity, trait theory focuses on the differences between individuals. Reportedly, Allport took all the adjectives in the English dictionary that described personality traits and categorized all these traits under three classes: Cardinal, Central, and Secondary.

According to this theory, cardinal traits are the dominant traits that mainly defines you as a person so much so that sometimes it becomes the trait that you become known for. An example of this is when someone who has a strong inclination to steal things is called a "kleptomaniac" or when someone who likes helping people a lot becomes known for their altruism. Basically, if people are asked what single word can be used to describe your behavior, that answer is most likely your cardinal trait.

Next, we have the central traits. These are the traits that come together to form the basic foundations of your personality. While they are not what you become known for, they are the traits that other people might use to describe you. Central traits are the traits present in everyone in varying degrees like loyalty, kindness, shyness, and intelligence.

Last, we have secondary traits which are specific and usually only come out under certain circumstances of situations like getting nervous when asked to sing in public. These traits don't always seem to fit someone's overall personality like when a friendly person suddenly gets angry over having to wait in line.

According to this theory, your lack of self-love generally comes from the combination of certain inborn traits that make you more prone to self-loathing or the lack of self-confidence. While this theory also suggests that personality traits can change over time through our experiences, they tend to be rather stable and consistent and even run in the family because it's more about our genetics.

It's an important perspective because if you think about it, many people go through the same experiences and share the same environment. No experience is ever truly unique to one person but somehow, people who share the same situation do not always share the same perspective and do not develop the same behaviors.

If you take a group of people and put them in the exact same situation, each of them will have a unique perspective regarding the situation. They will learn and react differently from each other, and their behaviors will still be different. For example, everyone who goes through a breakup experiences the same level of sadness. Some will recover from the emotional trauma faster than others and not everyone will deal with being single again in the same way. Some will get back into dating almost right away while some will spend years being single.

It can be said that according to this perspective, some of the people who bounce back right away may have been better-equipped with inborn traits that allow them to recover quickly from emotional pain while the others who take a much longer time to recover may have been more predisposed to be emotionally weaker. Of course, not all breakups are the same and I may be using an oversimplified example here, but it should make my point easier to understand.

However, a weakness in this perspective becomes obvious if we observe identical twins who grow up together. Identical twins come from the same fertilized egg cell that splits into two embryos, resulting in two babies who share an almost similar genetic makeup with just a few minor differences.

According to trait theory, identical twins should have the same psychology since they share almost the same exact genetic makeup. Their predispositions should be about the same and since they grew up together should behave in the same way.

This is not the case, based on my observations. I have two cousins who are identical twins and I also became friends with another pair of identical twins in college and in both cases, each of the twins has very different personalities. They also tend to make different choices and react differently from each other given the same situation.

While trait theory has its flaws, it's definitely a valid perspective that should not be ignored. However for our needs in the context of this book, trait theory is not something that I will put much stake on because I don't want you to think that you can't improve yourself because you are predisposed to self-loathing and I especially don't want you to use your genetics as an excuse to give up on yourself.

The Social Cognitive Theory

The social cognitive theory was founded by early psychologist Albert Bandura. It suggests that we learn by observing others and learning generally causes a change in our behavior. While trait theory suggests genetic predisposition as the largest factor in determining our behavior, social cognitive theory suggests that it's our social environment or the situation that plays the largest role in determining our personality.

According to this perspective, not only do we observe and imitate behaviors, but we also take into account the situation in which the behavior is performed and whether the behavior was rewarded or punished. It also suggests that we not only learn from what we directly observe in real time but that we also learn from the books we read or the movies we watch. In the simplest of terms, social cognitive theory says that our personality is developed and affected mainly by our environment. Our personalities are greatly influenced by the type of people we hang out with, the type of books we read or the movies we watch.

This suggests that children who grow up in loving, nurturing environments grow up to become kind adults because they are used to being treated with kindness by their parents while children who grow up with abusive parents are likely to become abusive parents themselves when they grow up.

As an example, let's go back to the story I told you at an earlier part of this book about my confidence in singing back when I was little. When I was little, I must have seen someone sing and after the performance, I saw that a lot of people were happy and gave the singer a lot of praise.

Because of this, I tried imitating the behavior by singing to my parents. Because my parents adored me and they wanted me to grow up with confidence, they praised me for it and because they praised me, I thought that I was a good singer and that I would get praised every time I sang. So, I ended up participating a lot in school presentations and would sing on stage, in front of an audience made up of teachers and other parents and because the socially-acceptable response to any child in this situation is to give praise, they would give me a round of applause and tell me that I'm a good singer even if I really wasn't.

When I grew up a little and tried to sing again, people weren't as generous with praise anymore and stopped praising me. Some would even tease me for it so instead of the usual reward, I instead started to get punished for singing. I did not want to be punished so I had to stop the behavior that gets me punished which was in this case, singing, so I stopped singing.

When it comes to the lack of self-love, this theory can explain the lack of self-love as the result of multiple bad experiences and a generally negative environment. Your self-loathing is a learned behavior. You don't love yourself because you learned not to love yourself by observing and experiencing a lot of negative things. The good news is that according to this theory just as you have learned not to love yourself, you can also learn to love yourself, and all you have to do is to change your environment.

I want to be honest and tell you that the theories I talked about are from the early days of psychology

and there are now many theories that better explain behavior. While many psychological approaches have been developed over the years, these serve as the foundation of modern psychology.

I reason that I am not trying to turn you into a psychologist. Human personality and behavior is a complicated thing and no single theory, old or new, can ever truly explain everything. These theories may be old, but they are enough to form a basic understanding of personality and behavior, and that's all that you need right now. More importantly, they're simple and easy to understand compared to many modern theories.

As I said, I'm not trying to turn you into a psychologist. I want to provide you with basic knowledge for me to create a background for the rest of the things that I'm trying to help you understand about yourself. I did not mention this before giving you the theories because I don't want you to have a bias against them before you learn about them. I still don't want you to disregard them now despite what I told you.

Biological Factors

If looking from the perspective of trait theory, genetics plays a significant role in determining our personality and behaviors. From this perspective, if you're not feeling enough love for yourself or if you're suffering from low self-esteem and a lack of confidence, the way you are born is to blame for your condition. You lack in those areas simply because you were predisposed to having them.

Also if you're not yet aware, some behaviors and mental illnesses are caused by chemical imbalances inside our bodies, particularly the chemical neurotransmitters that control and regulate brain activity. A popular neurotransmitter, for example, is Oxytocin which is sometimes referred to as the "Love hormone" because of how it influences pair bonding.

It's also believed to be the hormone that is majorly responsible for social interaction. It does a lot more than that of course, and there a lot more hormones that are known to affect behavior

As much as I would like to discuss hormones and their effects on behavior, I'll be honest and tell you outright that it's not my area of expertise. Additionally, issues that are caused by hormonal imbalances can only really be treated with medication and not something that you can solve by reading a book so we're not going to explore this line of thought any further.

Don't mistake this as me saying that biological factors are not important. All I'm saying is that if the root of the problem is in our biology then the solution is in modifying or controlling aspects of our biology and that's not something that I'm not equipped to discuss. If you believe that your issues may be hormonal or generally biological in nature then it's best to consult a doctor in order to get proper treatment.

I also have a person in my life who suffers from Schizophrenia and it's very difficult even for me as a trained therapist to manage his behavior without his medications so again, if you're suffering from a mental illness it's best to consult a physician first before considering other forms of treatment. However, I also want to acknowledge that many people don't want to take medicine if they don't have to. I also am aware that there are people who consider medicating as a form of weakness. Sometimes it may be the case but it's still best to not ignore medications as an option. Sometimes, just therapy is not enough and a little help using medications is the perfect working combination for people and that's completely fine.

That's it for the biological factors. As much as I would like to discuss them, it's neither my area of expertise nor is it something we can solve by reading a book so that's all I can say about the issue really. My recommendation is to try to seek treatment from a doctor if you feel like you need medication to deal with the problem.

This book will focus on the psychological and emotional part of things. We will attempt to explore your memories, your thought process, and your ideas in order to better understand yourself and to figure out the behavioral and experiential causes of your problem. I the same manner, we will explore how you can solve this problem using the tools you have inside you and I will attempt to guide you into learning how to love yourself using this book.

Upbringing and Environment

Each of us is unique and we are all built differently. Two people subjected to the same experience will be affected differently. We each interpret and react to experiences and events differently and though this can be attributed to the biological factors discussed earlier, it's also important to consider things like our upbringing and environment in terms of affecting the way we perceive ourselves and the world around us. The way we are raised, the culture we are exposed to, and the kind of environment where we were raised create in us a certain set of beliefs and biases that affect how we react to certain events and experiences.

Indoctrination

Sometimes it's just the way we are raised and what we have been taught by the people around us. As mentioned earlier in social cognitive theory, we learn through observation and everything we learn is taken in the context of the environment and the situation. Behaviors then become either reinforced or rooted out depending on the continuous exposure to the overall social environment and the response received when a behavior is performed.

When children grow up in an abusive environment, they develop certain psychological issues in response to the negative setting of their upbringing, which is usually a low sense of worth. Then they grow up and some of them may decide to start families of their own without having resolved these issues. Then, when these people with psychological or personality issues become parents, they may unintentionally treat their children in the same manner that they were treated for no other reason than because it was what they learned from their parents. Because of this, they imbue a low sense of worth to their children through their actions.

The word indoctrination itself is defined as the act of imbuing or teaching a biased point of view or opinion. While the word itself did not originally have a negative connotation, it is now used in association with religious cults specifically their brainwashing techniques to ensure the compliance of its members.

When taken in the context of social behavior, it can be taken to mean the teaching of a certain set of beliefs. While it's often unintentional, parents with issues tend to indoctrinate their children to view negative or abusive behavior as normal. The continued abuse is then taken by the child as what normal parents do. In turn, because we view our parents as the model for proper adult behavior, we tend to act the way they do. There is a theory that child molesters or sex offenders, in general, were themselves sexually abused as children. In the same manner, abusive people could have been abused as children. Based on this perspective a person with a low level of self-esteem, lack of self-confidence, and self-loathing is likely to have grown up with parents that share the same deficiencies.

I just want to be clear however that indoctrination is not exclusive to parent-child relationships. People with issues don't always have parents with issues. A person can have normal, loving parents but still get negatively indoctrinated by other adults especially when they are constantly exposed to these other adults. Sometimes it can even be the cultural norms and myths of the society we grow up in.

For example in some cultures, assertiveness is frowned upon and the importance of humility is emphasized. This is usually true with many Asian cultures where displays of self-confidence and celebrating success is considered inappropriate. In western society particularly in the American culture, bragging or touting your achievements is considered normal, appropriate, and even taken as a sign of having confidence in your abilities.

So, someone who was born and raised in Japan, for example, may be seen by an American as less-confident because they show humility and do not speak much of their achievements. On the other hand, the American may be seen as disrespectful and rude by a Japanese person for constantly bragging about his accomplishments.

Cultural aspects, therefore, must be taken into consideration when it comes to identifying the cause of low self-esteem or confidence. This may be the case for some immigrants who are unable to fully assimilate, as well as with children who are raised by at least one immigrant parent. In that parent's home country, displays of self-confidence and touting accomplishments may have been viewed negatively so that is how the parent raises their child. This, in turn, could create conflict inside the growing child if they are unable to find a way to synthesize or find their way around this conflicting environment.

Setting aside the parenting and cultural forms, indoctrination can sometimes come in the form of mass media. Sometimes when parents are unable to be present due to work, other responsibilities or when the parents simply lack the desire to provide their children with proper guidance, their children could get their social cues from the TV, from games, or from the internet.

Do you know how they say that playing violent games could cause violent tendencies in growing children? Have you paid attention to movie or tv ratings and the warnings about how "some scenes may be inappropriate" for children of a certain age group followed by "parental supervision is advised" or a similar statement? They're there for a reason. Sometimes a growing child is unable to differentiate between what they see in the media and in games, so an adult is needed to provide the necessary guidance.

Sometimes, low self-esteem or the lack of self-love can be due to the influence of the media. Children learn certain beliefs and behaviors impact their view of themselves and the world around them through their exposure to the media. They may learn to have unrealistic expectations of themselves that could lead to frustration and feelings of inadequacy. They might even learn to develop a negative worldview and this affects their sense of self-worth.

Regardless of the source or type, indoctrination plays a big role in how we view ourselves. Indoctrination shapes our view of the world around us and the way we develop our personalities and behaviors. The things we are constantly exposed to and told about ourselves and the social setting we grow up in influences how we see ourselves.

Predisposition to Self-Blame

We, humans, are blessed with a unique level of intelligence that other creatures on this planet cannot match. We can imagine different scenarios and predict future outcomes. We also have a considerable capacity to store memories for later review. This allows us to learn and adjust according to different situations quickly and to adapt to new environments quickly.

Compared to other predatory animals, we are physically weaker and slower, and we don't have unique physical features like the ability to camouflage ourselves to hide from other predators who may want to make a meal out of us. If the only factor for survival is physical fitness, humans would not be the dominant species on the planet and will probably be somewhere close to the bottom of the food chain.

Our high level of intelligence allows us to avoid danger by letting us predict and therefore avoid potential threats to our safety. Also, it has led us to have control or the environment through the tools we invent to make life easier. We can avoid harm because we have the ability to come up with solutions to problems both real and imagined.

This ability to imagine basically lets us come up with potential solutions to existing problems. We are in fact so smart that we can even come up with imagined problems that don't even exist in reality. This usually leads us to believe that we are in control of things and it's having this sense of control that gives us confidence. It's a manifestation of what we referred to earlier in psychoanalytic theory as the ego, and this ego desires to control.

Sometimes, due to certain situations, we start to lose control or at least feel like we are losing control. This perceived loss of control is unbearable for the ego and our mind lets us create what we call in psychological coping mechanisms or defense mechanisms in order to protect our fragile ego and let it maintain a sense of being in control.

When something goes wrong, we blame ourselves for not being able to do things right or for not knowing enough. We assign all the blame to ourselves and we make ourselves believe that everything wrong is our own fault, even the ones that are really outside of our control because it's somehow easier for us to hate ourselves than accept the fact that there are things that are outside of our power to control. We blame ourselves instead of accepting the fact that we had no control over something because blaming ourselves is much more bearable for our ego than to accept that we weren't in control.

For example, we sometimes like to believe that we can keep ourselves and our loved ones safe. We are in control of our safety and the safety of those we care about. When something bad happens like we get into an accident and we or our loved ones get hurt, we are faced with the idea that we were never in control in the first place, or that some things are simply beyond our control. The thought of not having full control of everything scares us so much that the idea of blaming ourselves feels much more bearable than the alternative. Basically, blaming ourselves is a defense mechanism to protect our ego because our ego cannot bear the idea of not being in control.

Correspondence Bias or Fundamental Attribution Error

All of us are curious by nature and we constantly try to understand the world around us. When something happens, we naturally try to find what caused this thing from happening. In psychology, this applies to our inherent need to figure out why people do the things they do. When we see someone do something, we try to figure out why they did it and this why is what we in the psychology world call attribution.

We have two types of attribution which are internal and external. Internal attribution is when we assume that the reason why someone does something is because of something about them. It can be their motivations, their personality, their beliefs, their emotions or their characteristics – basically something that comes from within that person. In simple terms, internal attribution explains that we behave the way we do because of how we are. External attribution, on the other hand, is the opposite. It's when we assume that the reason why someone does something is because of some external factor like their environment, upbringing, and the situation that they were in.

For example, when you get into a car accident and you think that it was because you were not being careful enough then you are making an internal attribution. On the other hand when you get into a car accident and you think that it's because it was raining and the road was slippery then you are making an external attribution. Another example is when you meet someone for the first time and they were being rude to you. When you think that this person is being rude because they're just not a good person then you are making an internal attribution.

On the other hand when you think that this person is being rude because they're tired or not in the mood out then you are making an external attribution. Having correspondence bias or fundamental attribution errors means you believe that everyone behaves based on personality all of the time and don't consider the idea that they may be just reacting to a given situation that you may not know about. In simple terms, you only use internal attributions to explain a person's behavior without giving any consideration about the situation or other things that might have influenced that person's behavior at the time. You don't believe that people behave differently under different situations.

An example of this is when a manager has to reprimand an employee and the employee believes that he is being reprimanded because the manager is a mean person. It's when he doesn't even try to consider what reasons the manager may have for issuing the reprimand. It might be because the employee's poor performance or a mistake that caused a big problem for the company but because of the correspondence bias of the employee, he fails to realize his own faults.

Essentially, people with a fundamental attribution bias are judgmental. It's usually because we are not always aware of a person's situation and all we really see is the person doing something. People with fundamental attribution bias just see a person behaving a certain way and automatically assume that it's just the way they are, and you make this assumption without even considering that there may be another reason for their behavior.

If the correspondence bias turns inwards or towards yourself, then you may start to get a distorted view of yourself. You start to berate yourself for not being able to accomplish a daily task or meet a daily goal because you think you were too lazy instead of considering your heavy workload. Whenever you make a mistake you just think that it's because you're simply too stupid to figure it out without even trying to consider that maybe there were other things that were in play. In a way, it's similar to self-blame because instead of accepting your limitations and seeing things objectively, you believe that a flaw in your character is to blame. It's always your fault and nobody else's.

V. Mental Illnesses and Psychological Conditions Associated with the Lack of Self-Love

Now that we have discussed a few things that can lead a mentally-sound person to loather themselves, I'm going to discuss some psychological conditions and mental illnesses that could lead to a lack of self-love. While some of these conditions can lead to a lack of self-love, the opposite can also be true in that some of these conditions can emerge as a result of the lack of self-love.

Generalized Anxiety Disorder

While it is normal to feel anxious when you're stressed or worried about things occasionally,

Generalized Anxiety Disorder is characterized by an ongoing and debilitating level of worry and anxiety. This disorder is when the level of anxiety or worry you feel is so great that it affects your performance of regular daily activities is hindered and causes problems in your relationships.

People with this generalized anxiety disorder are more susceptible to developing a low amount of self-esteem due to the nature of the problem. They worry about every little thing which drives down their level of self-confidence. They are unable to perform their job in an efficient manner especially when the symptoms manifest and so their self-respect takes a blow. Given that healthy self-esteem and self-respect are factors that contribute to self-love, generalized anxiety disorder can cause a person to love themselves less.

Inversely, a person with no self-love can develop generalized anxiety disorder because they lack confidence and feel helpless and uncertain about many things in their lives including their health and relationships.

Social Anxiety Disorder

While generalized anxiety disorder has a wide scope, social anxiety disorder is more specific in that the feelings of worry and uncertainty is directed towards social situations. People who suffer from social anxiety disorder experience excessive amounts of concern over being humiliated and embarrassed in front of other people. In many cases, the person who suffers from this condition becomes withdrawn and isolates themselves from other people because they fear being rejected or making a mistake and being made fun of.

Naturally, people with social anxiety disorder carry a low amount of self-love. They have problems connecting to other people which also hurts their self-esteem. They worry too much about embarrassing themselves and being rejected that they don't have enough confidence in themselves. They always feel weak and helpless in social settings and because of this, they find it hard to make friends. If you believe that you have this problem, I have a book titled Overcoming Social Anxiety which thoroughly discusses this particular issue. I also offer a free workbook that provides additional knowledge and exercises which would help to overcome social anxiety which you can find at my website. I also offer a full blog where I touch issues on self-love and social anxiety and provide encouragement and inspiration which you can all get for free at **jen.green**.

Body Dysmorphic Disorder

Body dysmorphic disorder is a mental illness which concerns the way we see our physical form. It's when you're extremely concerned or bothered by a certain part or parts of your body. It's normal to feel insecure or concerned for example, about being a little overweight or if you have a visible scar. It becomes a disorder when you think about it so much that it consumes your thoughts and when these thoughts start affecting your behavior and relationships negatively.

It's highly subjective in a way that sometimes the flaw that causes concern may be something that only the person suffering from it sees the problem and while other people don't. It may be surprising to you that bodybuilders and some fitness buffs have it. You might wonder how people who look like Greek god statues have this issue and it's really simple: a lot of them started out not being happy with the way their bodies looked at some point, perhaps feeling like their not muscular enough or they're not as fit as they should be in their heads.

Given that this disorder affects the way you perceive yourself, it's easy to say that it also affects self-love as you get the feeling that you're not enough or that you're not doing enough. In some extreme cases, people risk their health by taking steroids or spend a lot of money on expensive plastic surgery to fix their perceived problem.

Anorexia Nervosa

Anorexia nervosa is similar to body dysmorphic disorder in that it's when a person is extremely concerned about their physical form. People who suffer from this illness look at themselves in the mirror and see themselves as being fat or obese.

The significant difference is that anorexia nervosa is more of an eating disorder. They believe that they're too fat so they go through extreme dieting, even going as far as starving themselves to death. If left untreated people suffering from this disorder die of malnutrition and develop other illnesses due to the lack of sustenance.

Another difference between anorexia and body dysmorphic disorder is that people with anorexia see themselves as overweight only and they're really not concerned about specific parts of their body. In body dysmorphic disorder it may not just be an issue of being fat but it can be a certain scar or birthmark or a specific part of the body that the person with this disorder considers a disfigurement.

Borderline Personality Disorder

People with borderline personality disorder have problems in managing their emotions and their responses to these emotions. It's characterized by ongoing mood swings and a constant feeling of uncertainty about themselves and their role in society. People with this disorder tend to view things in extremes like everything is good or everything is bad. They also tend to have constantly changing opinions of people and situations in such a way that a person who they think is a friend today may be an enemy the next without any apparent reason.

Building lasting relationships can be a challenge for people with this disorder due to the constantly shifting nature of the person's mood and the instability of the person's behavior towards other people. People suffering from this disorder may also engage in risky behaviors such as engaging in unsafe sex or drug abuse in times of elevated mood. They may also easily become angry and go into fits of rage over seemingly minor reasons or mistrust people due to an extreme fear of people's intentions.

Depression

Depression is characterized by a persistent feeling of sadness and loss of interest. It's often a common thing these days to say that someone is "depressed" when they're feeling down or sad and while depression is characterized by sadness, but it's a deeper more prolonged period of sadness that affects a person's behavior, health, and relationships. People suffering from depression may feel no interest and display a lack of enthusiasm for performing even their day-to-day activities. They may not feel pleasure in activities that generally bring joy and excitement such as sex, games, and sports. Their sense of self-worth is also significantly reduced that they feel worthless and may have recurring thoughts of suicide. Sometimes it may even be accompanied by physical symptoms such as lack of energy, insomnia, and specific aches and pains that have no apparent cause.

Depression is a serious issue and should not be taken lightly because the consequences if left untreated, can be severe. People suffering from depression often need to take medications along with psychotherapy. If you feel depressed and have thoughts of committing suicide, please call the suicide hotline 1-800-273-8255 if you're from the US or you can talk to a loved one or a close friend.

I have lost a good friend due to depression once, so this is a sensitive subject for me personally so again, if you suffer from depression please talk to someone you trust when you're having suicidal thoughts. Seek medical treatment from a psychiatrist and search for a therapist near you who you feel comfortable with. If you're reading this book right now and you have had suicidal thoughts please put this book down and talk to a friend or a loved one and seek medical attention. You do not have to suffer this alone help is available if you try to seek it.

Sometimes I still feel regret over losing him as I never knew he had depression. I wish he had talked to me about it. He must have felt so sad and alone, and he didn't see that there were a lot of us who cared about him. As a final note on this issue, committing suicide to escape your pain and misery only transfers that pain and misery to the people who care about you that you leave behind. Please, if you feel like ending your life for any reason, please seek help.

Post-Traumatic Stress Disorder

Post-traumatic stress disorder or PTSD as its name implies is a mental disorder that results from experiencing a traumatic event. People who suffer from this illness often find themselves unable to get over the memories of the traumatic events they have suffered that it affects the way they think, the way they behave, and the way they treat the people around them. They can feel like the world is a dangerous place and they start acting overprotective and become extremely concerned with their security. My uncle always kept all windows covered because he was afraid of being seen through the window by a sniper.

PTSD also causes difficulty going to sleep, and when they do get sleep, they often have vivid and terrifying dreams about the traumatic events they suffered. They're also sometimes hyperalert that they get startled easily like they're always on edge and get upset over seemingly small things and end up with angry outbursts.

VI. Learning To Love Yourself

Is it Okay to Go on With Life Without Loving Myself?

The answer is both complicated and straightforward. The simple answer is that without loving yourself, you'll keep feeling the way you are feeling right now. There are a lot of people who go on with their lives never realizing that their problems come from a deep, unrecognized self-loathing. They have this inner critic that keeps telling them how badly they are doing and it never ends. They simply accept that they are below other people and go on not ever feeling that they are enough and they seem to be living normal lives.

So, it's okay, right? This is where it's complicated. I mean if a lot of people go through life not even realizing that they don't love themselves but keep on with their lives. It's not like love is needed for our bodies to function right? It's not like food, drink or air. A lot of people live their lives not ever experiencing being in loving relationships. You probably know a few sad, old people who live alone with no one in their lives. Is that what you want for yourself?

Here's the thing: You got this book because you know that you can't keep being the way you are right now. You want things to change, you want your life to improve, you want to experience how it is to actually be happy and content with yourself. Those are things that you may never achieve if you don't do something to fix the situation. You realized that the problem is that you don't love yourself enough and that it needs to be fixed.

You're probably tired of not ever feeling like you're enough. Your inner critic keeps nagging at you, second-guessing all your decisions and you keep looking back and reviewing your memories for things that you could have done differently if only you knew what you know now. You're tired of constantly feeling ashamed. It's why you're still reading right? Not loving yourself leaves you open to a lot of psychological issues like the ones I mentioned in the section about mental illnesses related to the lack of self-love. Your physical health may also suffer because you may not be taking good care of yourself. Your social life will suffer, you'll keep hanging out with the wrong people, and you'll find it hard to connect with the people who may actually give your life meaning.

That's why it's important to learn how to love yourself the right way. Loving yourself means living a meaningful life. Loving yourself means happiness and fulfillment. Loving yourself leads to building healthy and meaningful relationships. That is what you're missing out on if you decide to go on with life without loving yourself. So, is it okay to go on with life without loving yourself?

Self-Concept and Motivation

So far I've focused on factors that shape human personality and behavior and how they all contribute to how people are more likely to respond to certain events or situations. These include your genetic makeup and your hormonal activity, your upbringing and environment. We have also discussed psychological theories on how behavior and personality develop and how it affects your overall disposition. In short, we have focused on the things that predispose you to self-loathing. Now, we're going to discuss external factors, which are essentially your experiences. While the way your parents treated you as a child counts as experience, I'm treating it as an entirely separate category because for most people, self-loathing does not manifest or become a problem until later in life, specifically around the late youth or adult stage.

So far what we have discussed is all about predisposition which is in a nutshell, the things that determine how you are likely to react when things happen to you. Now, we are going to discuss motivation. Motivation in simple terms is what makes you likely to do things. You want to love yourself. You want to be a better person. That was your motive for getting and reading this book.

We start life as selfish creatures. As a baby, you didn't care about how your parents lost sleep over your crying in the middle of the night. You cried because you wanted to express hunger or discomfort and that's it. You didn't care how your food was made or anything else other than that you're no longer hungry once you're fed. As you grew up, you started to see yourself as part of a larger world and you started to understand that your actions affect others. You didn't see any problems with you until you started to see how the way you are affects your relationship with other people.

Sometimes you just don't realize that you are lacking in self-love until you start building lasting relationships. As a child or during your early youth you usually lack the necessary social context to realize that your problem is a lack of self-esteem and confidence. Your parents don't always recognize that there is a problem with your self-esteem as a child because it's normally assumed that children will eventually grow out of their shyness and are expected to mature and change and they wouldn't be wrong. You go through changes as you age both because your body changes in composition and activity, and you go through experiences that develop your sense of self.

In trying to learn to love yourself, it's important to, of course, understand the concept of self. What are you? How did you become you? Why are you the way you are? While we may have already touched this in discussing behavior and personality, it's still not complete until we discuss the concept of self because in order to love yourself, you first have to know yourself and that's what we'll discuss in the following section.

The Hierarchy of Needs

The psychologist Abraham Maslow came up with a hierarchy of needs in order to describe how a person achieves self-actualization. Self-actualization is defined as a person's motive to reach their full potential. In other words, self-actualization is the feeling of being complete and for the purposes of this book, being complete means loving yourself completely for what complete person does not love themselves?

You've probably seen Maslow's hierarchy in the form of a pyramid where at the bottom is physiological needs, followed by safety needs, then love and belonging, esteem, then on top is self-actualization. According to this theory, in order to meet a higher-leveled need, the needs below it must first be met. In order to gain self-actualization, a person has to first have a healthy level of self-esteem. In order for a person to work on gaining esteem, they first have to feel loved and have a sense of belonging. In order to work on feeling loved and have a sense of belonging, one must first feel safe. In order to work on feeling safe, one must first meet their physiological needs. In simple terms, physiological needs are the basic needs – food, water, air, etc. - The things you need to survive. They are placed at the bottom of the pyramid because these needs are the foundation for all other needs. All other needs are secondary to the need to live. It's the primary motivation for all human behavior because before you can worry about anything else, you first have to make sure that you'll keep on living.

Once you have ensured your survival by meeting your physiological needs, the next thing you need is to have security or to feel safe. Naturally, you're motivated to protect yourself and your loved ones. You may be able to keep living by eating, drinking, and breathing but you have to ensure that you can continue living by keeping yourself and your food, water and air safe.

Love and belonging is the next level and is where we are going to start working for you to learn to love yourself in this book. Love and belonging needs are what motivates you to seek the approval of others, to have friends, and to feel that you matter. You can feel full and completely safe, but just being full and safe is not enough to make you happy right?

Esteem needs are defined by the need for status and respect and it's the area that we are primarily going to work on in this book. We have the desire to be accepted and valued by others, so we do things like act in certain ways in order to gain recognition from others. Interestingly, we also desire to be accepted and valued by ourselves and that's where learning to love yourself plays an important part and that's what this book is all about.

Self-Concept Theory

Self-Concept Theory is pioneered by Carl Rogers and in this theory, he puts emphasis on our perceptions of ourselves and how we see ourselves in the context of our relationships and how we affect the world around us. He calls this the self-concept, which is essentially how you would answer the question "Who am I?"

Your self-concept is important because the way you perceive yourself greatly affects self-love. If you have a healthy self-concept, it's easier for you to love yourself. While Rogers lists the components of self-concept as self-image, self-esteem or self-worth and the ideal self, I found it necessary to reclassify each component into self-image, self-worth, and congruence vs. incongruence in which congruence vs. incongruence results from the overlap between two of the factors that determine self-image.

Self-Image

Self-image in simple terms is how we see ourselves. How do you see yourself? What kind of person are you according to you? What do you think are the things that make you unique? Essentially, self-image is your beliefs about yourself, and these beliefs are what shapes your identity. It doesn't necessarily have to be based on reality.

The ideal self, on the other hand, is what you wish you would be. What do you want to be? Who do you want to be? The ideal self represents what you wish you could be. It provides you with a goal and it's where your motivation to change comes from. In terms of self-love, it's your idea of what kind of person you'll become once you learn to love yourself. It's the reason that you're seeking help. It's what motivated you to get this book and read it.

The looking glass self is what you think others see you as. How do you think others see you? What are you to these people? How would other people describe you if they were asked about you? The looking glass self does not necessarily have to be based on reality because you can't really know what others think about you so you try to make an assumption or an estimation. In terms of self-love, it's when you think that other people don't respect you or look down on you. You want to learn to love yourself because you want to be able to act in a way that lets other people think that you're worthy of their attention and respect.

Your real self is basically the areas where your self-image and your looking glass self, match. In terms of self-love, it's when you think that you're not worthy of respect and people don't respect you. When you think that you're not worthy of anyone's attention and people ignore you then that's your real self. Rogers further expands Maslow's ideas, particularly about self-actualization. According to him, each person has in him the potential to achieve their goals in life. Everyone can fulfill their wishes and desires and self-actualization is if and when these goals are met or these wishes and desires are achieved.

He believes that all humans are inherently good and creative. He rejects the deterministic nature of other theories on personality and behavior like psychoanalysis. He does not believe that people are predisposed to certain behaviors and instead holds that all humans have just one single motive and it's our desire to attain self-actualization. He believes that in order to attain self-actualization, all that a person needs is to be given the right conditions and be put in the right set of situations in order to achieve their goals.

According to him, there can never be a single formula that determines how people behave or how personality develops. Instead, he believes that each of us is truly unique and it's our individual circumstances and experiences that determine how our personalities develop and that our behaviors are entirely dependent on how we perceive ourselves and the given situation.

While he disagrees with the psychoanalytic approach, he does agree with Freud in the importance of a person's childhood. He believes that as children we only have just two basic needs that shape our self-perception or how we think of ourselves. First is self-worth and the other one is positive regard.

Self-Worth

Self-worth is the term used to describe how we regard ourselves. It's how we value ourselves. Rogers believes that self-worth is primarily developed from early childhood and is the result of the interaction between the child and his or her parents and later in life, the interactions with significant others.

A person who develops a low amount of self-worth may not be as confident about themselves and may not be open to accepting the idea that life is not always going to go their way. They may fear and avoid challenges in life and may be mistrustful of other people. On the other hand, a person who develops a high level of self-worth is more confident and willing to take on challenges in life. They may also be more open to accepting that life comes with difficulties and unhappiness, and they may be more open to other people as well.

Positive regard is essentially the approval we get from other people, particularly our parents. It has to do with how we are valued and how other people make us feel about ourselves. He further classifies positive regard as conditional and unconditional.

Conditional positive regard is when the recognition, approval or praise we get as children depends on our actions. It's when you get praised for doing something that your parents or other adults think is good behavior. This gives the child the impression that love is a conditional thing. They will start believing that they will only be loved if they act according to how their parents want them to act. Too much of this type of regard could eventually lead to the child growing up as a person who constantly seeks approval from other people.

Unconditional positive regard is when the recognition, approval or praise we get is not dependent on our actions. In simple terms, it's unconditional love. This lets the child know that they are free to try new things and that they don't have to be afraid of making mistakes. The problem with unconditional positive regard is that when it's too much, a child can grow into a person who does not care about the consequences of their actions.

According to this approach, a person who experiences more of the unconditional type of positive regard is more likely to reach self-actualization because they develop a better sense of self-worth. Additionally, the concept of congruence is introduced.

Congruence Vs. Incongruence

Congruence is when your ideal self and your experiences match. If you remember what we discussed earlier, self-image is how you view yourself while the ideal self is how you wish things to be. Normally, we would want to behave according to our self-image because we want to match the ideals that we set for ourselves. We also want our ideal selves or our experiences and feelings to be consistent with this self-image. Therefore, the closer our self-image is from our ideal self, the more congruent we are and the higher our sense of self-worth becomes.

In relation to loving yourself, the theories of self-concept and motivation should help not only in determining why you don't love yourself, but help guide you into your road to fixing yourself. Right now, there is probably an incongruence between your self-image and your ideal self.

Most likely, your ideal self is one who feels a sense of completion. You want to feel respected by the people around you and you want to make genuine connections with other people and create lasting relationships. You want to stop feeling that emptiness inside that keeps wanting to be filled. You want to be truly happy and content on the inside and not just on the surface. You want to stop wearing a mask of happiness while feeling dead inside.

So, you know what you want but your current state is not that. You feel a sense of emptiness and you're not happy inside. You want people to love you for what you really are but you're afraid of showing them your true self because you're scared that the real you is not something they would want to see. You're tired of pretending to be okay and you're tired of being a spectator in your own life and you want to take control. That's an incongruence. It frustrates you and you want to change. Your goal is your ideal, and you want to reach that ideal and you recognize that what you need is to improve yourself.

First, congratulations, you are already on your way to recovery. You were able to recognize and accept that you have a problem and you have also figured out that you need to fix this problem. How is that a good thing, you may ask at this point. Let me explain.

Most people who don't love themselves have learned to accept their feelings and situations and have decided to just keep pretending that everything is okay. You've probably met a lot of them. Actually, you were, in the beginning, one of them. You used to feel empty, and you used to hate the way you are and what did you tell yourself then?

Was it something like "It's okay. One day I'll find someone..." – Like your happiness and sense of completion was just a matter of finding the right person to come into your life. You believed that someone would come along to make you feel complete so you may have rushed from relationship-to-relationship because you thought that this new person is the one. Then, the honeymoon phase is over and you find that this person wasn't the one all along so you drive them away and find another person and again believe that this person is the one.

If not that, then what you might have done is hold off from getting into a relationship with anyone because you're waiting for that special someone. You have a set of ideas in your head like a checklist that someone needs to complete in order for you to tell that they are exactly the person you need. Worse, you might have just gone with anyone who showed you some interest because you think that eventually, this person might turn out to be the one if given time. Before you know it, you're just making accommodation after accommodation because you feel like this person is the best shot you got at becoming complete. Regardless of how you did it, you were wrong from the start in thinking that your happiness depended on another person. You were wrong all along in believing that you needed someone else to give you a sense of completion.

Maybe it wasn't that. Maybe instead of trying to find someone, you instead have accepted your lot in life. You made yourself believe that everyone is just like you – pretending to be okay while feeling empty inside. You think that the emptiness is a normal thing for everyone and so you just try to go and pretend like everyone else. So, you made friends with people who also have holes in them and you like to hang out and talk about how empty you are inside. You feel a sense of belonging which is a good thing, but you already decided that feeling empty is normal. You may have tried drugs together with these friends because whenever you're high, everything is okay. You may not have done drugs, but you only ever feel like these other empty people are the only people in the world who can ever really accept you and you make yourself completely dependent on them for support. Misery certainly loves company. Don't get me wrong, it's great to have friends who are like you but you're ignoring the main problem here. What happens if your friends move on? How do you feel when they're not with you? Are they going to be there for you forever?

Going back to my main point, you're already on your way to fixing the problem. I can tell because you're not accepting that the way you feel, not loving yourself, is something that you can't do anything about. You realized that you have a problem, you identified the root of this problem, and you decided to try and do something about it and that is worthy of praise. So again, congratulations. We have tried to identify the things that you may have that cause you to lack self-love and at this point, I hope you have a clear idea of what may have caused your self-loathing. It's now time to find out how to fix you.

First, let's start with a list of quick and somewhat easy fixes. Now I don't know you as an individual, so I can't give you a specific regimen. So, I'll list a few things that I recommend you do regularly. These things don't require much thinking and are effective when done consistently. Depending on your level of self-hate and depending on your needs and other factors, these may be all you need to fix yourself.

After this list of quick fixes, I'm going to try to give you a few techniques used by therapists like me. Now before you start expecting big things, I have to first tell you a few important things. First is that we therapists needed to go through years of school and there is no way that I can teach you everything you need to know in a single book. Second, I know that you were probably expecting some awesome secret techniques that only therapists know and that after doing these secret techniques you'll be fixed. It that's what you thought or expected then you would be wrong. Nothing about what we do is a secret. In fact, you can find almost every tool we use online for free. So what makes therapists special and why do we spend years studying if anyone can just lookup solutions and techniques online and use them? The short answer is that it's knowing about which specific techniques to use. Think of it as going to a doctor versus going to WebMD. You can find almost every disease, symptom, cause and treatment available for free from WebMD but how can you make sure that you have the right diagnosis? What if you had a headache, went on to look it up online and found that a headache may be caused by many different things? What if your headache was just a headache? How can you tell which treatment is best? Never mind that you need a doctor to write you a prescription for most medications, how can you be sure that you got the right diagnosis and the right treatment from reading a thousand things about a headache online?

So again, let's go back to me giving you techniques. I'll do my best to give a set of techniques that are not too specific, something that could work for most people. I hope it's enough to at least point you in the right direction. I'm going to give you a major secret though and it should really help you a lot.

Starting The Process of Loving Yourself

While the concept of self-love is complicated, starting the process of learning to love yourself is not that complicated. For now, I will give you a few simple steps and you probably already know most of these. These are the quick fixes that I told you about earlier and I won't be surprised if you had already started doing them even before you got this book. If you have tried these and they haven't worked for you, then maybe what you need is to give them another try and this time, try to be consistent. Let's start!

1. Figure Out the Things That Will Make You Feel Good and Do Them Regularly

What will make you feel good right now as in, right this moment? Maybe you like ice cream, and there's some ice cream in the fridge. Go ahead and put down this book, walk to the refrigerator and help yourself to some ice cream. Maybe there's a song that you like, go ahead and listen to it. Maybe watching a good movie will cheer you up, why not watch it?

The point of this exercise is to think of the things that you can do now that will make you feel good but won't have any negative consequences. What I mean is that for example, if you have diabetes and your doctor has told you to stay away from the sweet stuff then don't pick that. For now, stick with the small, simple and achievable things that will bring you even just a tiny bit of pleasure. No need for big, complicated moves. Go ahead and enjoy yourself however, just to be sure, don't do anything that you might regret later.

Remember, what we want here are small and easy amounts of happiness that we don't have to ever regret doing. Eat some good food, pet your dog, play with your kids, anything that's within reach right now that will make you happy do it. Do these things regularly. Let yourself have a little fun, you deserve it.

A lot of small yet regular doses of happiness can be very beneficial for starting the process of loving yourself. Sometimes we get so busy with our jobs and obligations that we forget all about these little things that we can do to feel good. It's funny how often we forget about these small pleasures in life because we get caught up in going after the big ones. What I do myself is I have pints of Chocolate Fudge Brownie ice cream that I keep in the freezer, reserved for days when I feel extra stressed or when my day isn't going so well. If I need a little dose of joy, I walk to our fridge and get myself a good serving, and it makes me happy. This is of course aside from taking care of my kids which is a joy, as well as playing video games with my husband almost every night as a form of bonding.

How can this help with learning to love yourself you ask? Simple. You're rewarding yourself. You're giving yourself small rewards and YOU DESERVE THEM. You're pampering yourself. You're giving yourself the permission to make yourself happy and that's important to your mental well-being.

So again, think of all the small and easy things that will give you pleasure and go do them.

2. Whenever You Find Yourself Starting to Think of Sad Thoughts, Divert Your Thoughts into Happy Things

Okay, this one can be a little tricky. Some thoughts can be hard to ignore, and well, there are things that we have to think about and solve but in this case, I'm talking about the memories that bother you. The things that you really regret but can't do anything about. The things that are final and can only be fixed with a time machine that you don't have.

This one is right up my alley. I used to always be bothered by my past mistakes. I used to think about past relationships and regret having been into some of them. I think about all those wrong guys that I should never have been with in the first place. I think of all the signs that I should have noticed. I remember everything wrong about those relationships and I regret all the pain and grief that I could have avoided and all the things that I could have gained if I hadn't been with these men and it makes me cringe. Some of them I used to regret losing. I would think about what I did wrong or wonder what I might have done that caused the relationship to end.

Sometimes it's just memories of tripping in front of class back in elementary, of being in front of the class and freezing up because I got too embarrassed to have all my classmates' eyes on me, stuff like that. The common factor among all these thoughts and memories is that it's all in the past. No amount of thinking can ever fix anything. No amount of time spent thinking about them will ever affect what I am in the present and what I could be in the future, and that's what I want you to realize.

While sometimes we get overcome by some powerful thoughts that don't seem to leave us alone, we can to a certain degree control what goes on in our heads, especially when it comes to the things we remember. When you find yourself starting to think of painful memories, you can try diverting your thoughts into happier ones.

What I learned to do is to create a "happy place" in my head where I can go whenever I find myself thinking of painful things. Mine is a particular spot in a beach in Pacific Grove, California where I used to always go with my cousin whenever we need to vent. In my head I just go there and picture myself sitting on a rock, listening to the waves crash and watching a sea otter slam shellfish against its belly. It's soothing for me.

Try it. It can be based on a real place, one that you've visited before or it can be a place that you create yourself. There's really no limit to what you can imagine. Just create that place and whenever painful thoughts start creeping up, close your eyes and take yourself to that magical place where it's beautiful and relaxing where nothing can hurt you or bother you.

Alternatively, you can divert your thoughts on happy memories from your childhood or in the recent past. It doesn't even have to be memories or a happy place but instead, it can be your plans for the future. Think instead of what you want to be. Imagine yourself being in the moment that you achieve your goals where your life is finally in order and you are where you want to be and you are who you want to be. This should help keep you motivated to work towards your goal of learning how to love yourself.

Whatever it is you decide to divert your thoughts into is entirely up to you as long as it helps you to not think about the things that bring you pain but can never change or do anything about. The less you think about these painful and negative thoughts, the more you can focus on seeing your own awesomeness and appreciate yourself.

3. Think of Your Goals and Work Towards Reaching Them

I'm using the word "Goals" here as a blanket term for all things that you need to accomplish as well as all the things that you want to achieve in both the long term and the short term. This can be the goal of learning how to love yourself the right way as I assume it's what you want when you got this book, or it can be a small goal like just making dinner or even cleaning the house.

First, let's focus on the small day-to-day tasks. Just find your flow. Think about all the things you need to accomplish for today. If you find yourself not having a clear daily goal, just look around and try to look for things that you can clean and organize. Look for things that you can fix or modify. Sometimes just being productive helps a lot in avoiding the negative thoughts that your inner critic tells you.

It can also give you the pleasure of actually accomplishing something. The keyword here is productive, not busy. There's a huge difference between being busy and being productive. You can always be busy without accomplishing anything useful or meaningful. It's always best to have a certain goal in your mind and then start working towards it.

For my daily goals, I usually make it a point to write at least a thousand-word article per day that I can use for either my current book or for a possible future book. I also subdivided our house into four sections: the back and front yard, the bedrooms, the living room, and kitchen, and the bathrooms. I make it a daily goal to clean and organize each of these sections every weekday while my kids are at school. This way I keep myself productive, and I get a sense of accomplishment daily which aside from the actual benefits of having a clean and organized home, also helps with my self-esteem.

As for long-term goals, what do you want to accomplish? Is there a job position that you want to reach? Is there an amount of money you want to be making by a certain point? My husband is the expert on setting these long-term goals and has taught me a technique where he breaks down larger goals into smaller manageable chunks.

If I haven't mentioned it before, my husband is a self-employed online seller. He's actually the one who encouraged me to try to write books and publish them on Amazon. What he does is he takes a huge goal like "make a million dollars in one year" and creates a flowchart where he breaks it down to quarterly, monthly, weekly, and daily goals. In no way are we millionaires yet but I appreciate how he has actual goals and is a good provider for the family.

Anyway, the way he explains it to me is that sometimes a goal looks like it's a hugely difficult task like making a million dollars in one year. If you think about your current situation then making a million dollars one year from now doesn't look easy.

However, if you break down one million dollars into twelve monthly chunks then it becomes about $83,000 a month. Then if you divide it in thirty days, you have to make about $2,800 per day.

I don't know exactly how my husband does it, but it makes sense doesn't it? Any huge goal may seem like it's impossible if you look at it as a whole but when you break it down into smaller pieces and focus on accomplishing one small piece at a time, eventually you will reach your goal without even noticing it.

Sometimes it's the feeling of being overwhelmed or the feeling that we can never achieve our impossible goals that gets us down. Sometimes it's the feeling that we never accomplish anything useful that makes us lose self-respect. Well, here's a way for you to feel accomplished. Apply my husband's method. Think about your dreams, think about what you want to become one day, set a reasonable time frame to accomplish it, then break it down into manageable daily tasks and start working towards accomplishing each daily task.

Being productive this way has the benefit of gaining you self-respect because you get closer to achieving your goals and it also serves as a much better alternative to just feeling hopeless and doing nothing to improve yourself. At the very least, it provides a distraction from thinking negative thoughts and it brings you a sense of accomplishment.

4. Collect and Store Happy Thoughts and Experiences in a Journal

Journaling or keeping a diary is something that I never really got into until later in college. I always thought that writing daily experiences is a waste of time. It just wasn't my thing. However, my opinion changed one day when we were asked to create a special one-month journal as a project.

We were asked to simply write down everything positive that happened during each day. It didn't have to be long and detailed, it just had to be a short description of things that made us happy each day. It could be a random compliment, a thing that we saw, or something we did as long as it gave us even a little amount of happiness. Then, at the end of the month, we were all asked to read through the journal we made and write down an essay about "life."

It was a fun experience. It made me realize that good things happen to you daily if you only care to pay attention to them. It's easy to forget about a random compliment from a stranger or a simple video clip of cute animals that you saw at some point during the day but if you keep a record of it you start to see that life is full of these little joys that you forget about because well, they're small and quick.

So, I'm going to try asking you to do the same. Try to keep a journal of happy thoughts. Just write down anything good that happens to you in a notebook or on your computer. It doesn't have to be anything fancy as long as you have the ability to write down these things and are able to separate them from day-to-day.

Sometimes we feel like nothing good ever happens to us like we don't deserve to have anything nice. It's because when you lack self-love, you tend to focus on the negative things and you completely forget to notice and appreciate the small good things that happen in your day.

5. Have Good Internal Conversations with Yourself

You know that inner critic of yours? It's a construct that you built either consciously or subconsciously and you have programmed it to criticize you. Now, how about you construct an inner friend who will tell you nice things about yourself? Does that sound good?

Think about it. Your inner critic is something you made. It's probably not something you consciously built but it's there and nobody else could have put it there. It reminds you all about the things you did wrong, it tells you how you should have or could have done things, and it's there to second-guess your decisions. Unlike many of my fellow psychologists however, I don't believe that it's an entirely bad thing.

If it's just the mild form, listening to your inner critic can actually be beneficial. It keeps you grounded and at the very least, it helps you with making decisions because it's there to remind you how bad things could get and it's there to try to prevent you from getting hurt. It's sort of a mental defense mechanism. It only really becomes your enemy when it becomes strong and so negative that it simply brings you down.

So, my solution is this. Create an inner friend. Try to think of how you are to your friends. Think about what you want your friends to be and become that person to yourself. If that doesn't make sense then let's put it this way. What do you tell a friend when they screw up or when they're feeling down or when things aren't going so well? Now when you screw up or feeling down or when things aren't going well for you, just tell yourself what you would tell your friends.

It's simple right? It's not just telling yourself that you love yourself or that you're awesome in front of the mirror but actually practicing the art of having a positive internal conversation. Try it out, it works wonders for your self-esteem.

6. Make A Conscious Decision to Change to Yourself and Follow Through

When did you figure out that your problem was not having enough love for yourself? What made you decide to finally do something about it? You must have noticed at some point that you're no longer happy with how things are going, did some looking around, and found that maybe what you need is a healthy dose of love and self-respect and that's why you eventually got this book right? Congratulations, you've already done this step. All you need now is to follow through.

The problem sometimes is that we realize the problem and decide to make a change, but then when things start to be hard and complicated, we ourselves want to give up and decide to just settle for how things were before. It's normal to be like that. Any major change requires a lot of adjustments and actual work. You can't expect to simply decide to change and then instantly have it occur.

It's said that the hardest part of ending something is having to start all over again and it's true in this situation. You've probably spent some time hating yourself or at least not loving yourself enough. You're used to the situation and you're used to the uneasiness that comes with it. You've probably given up at some point and decided to just accept your lot in life. Then, you thought that maybe you should give it another shot and you aren't wrong in deciding to do so. Loving yourself has its unique benefits.

Whenever we are challenged by something new, the easiest thing to do seems to be to just throw in the towel and give up. The old and familiar usually starts looking like the better option than diving into the unknown and hoping for things to improve once things start to get difficult. It's human nature. We learn to adapt to the current situation and it becomes what's normal, even if this normal isn't really what we want.

I understand completely. I spent most of my childhood and teen years with social anxiety and self-doubt. I got so used to it that it no longer surprised me to find that I had no real friends other than my cousins who are sort of your friends by default. They would introduce me to some new people and everything works out in the beginning but then when my issues arise, these new people just end up getting bored with me and eventually forget about me.

I got so used to it that back in high school I just learned to accept it and did not even try to let other people in. I didn't even give myself a chance to open up and get close to others. I didn't give others a chance to get to know me either because I just assume from the start that these people will just get bored with me eventually, so I didn't even try hanging out or talking to them anymore.

While I did have relationships with a couple of guys in high school, I was never really comfortable and felt like I was just being used and I was just mostly there in an attempt to fit in. I thought that maybe these guys would help me open up, and I depended on them and expected them to change me. Of course, it never worked. You can't expect other people to cover the hole you have inside you. It has to be you who fixes you.

If I hadn't run into the guidance counselor back then I wouldn't have known that my problem had a root cause. He made me realize that what I needed was to learn to love and appreciate myself. I knew there was something wrong with me but I didn't think that it was something that I could fix. All that time I just thought that it was really just how I am and that there is nothing else that I could do so I should just accept it. I gave up on myself and did not think to even ask for help.

While I did try to be sociable and forced myself at first to try to hang out with my popular cousin's friends, I never really showed them what I could do and I always just took a passive role because I let myself become afraid of doing something to make them dislike me. It's ironic because in the end, being passive made them think of me as a boring person which drove them away. I understood though, I mean who would want to hang out with someone who doesn't have an opinion and just keeps silent most of the time? My cousin kept on introducing me to new people but eventually, everyone already knew about me, and I also did not make an effort to try to get close to these new people.

My cousin tried to help me, but I never gave myself a chance. I gave up and stopped trying and it's one of my biggest what if's. My cousin was one of the popular girls and she really tried. I realize now that I'm not as unattractive as I thought I was and my mid-college life was filled with fun experiences. I used to wonder if I could have been popular in high school like my cousin if I just kept hanging out with the friends she introduced to me and really expressed myself. I guess I'll never know.

So, follow through. It's probably not going to be easy especially when you've spent a long time loathing yourself and ignoring your needs. Keep practicing everything I'm telling you to do, even the small seemingly pointless ones. It's only really difficult in the beginning and don't let yourself give up because of the frustration.

7. Learn to Appreciate Yourself

Remember that part I told you about doing something that makes you feel good and that part about having good internal conversations? Let's combine those two and take it a step further. How about actually learning to thank yourself whenever you do something that feels good? Whenever you serve yourself some of that ice cream, thank yourself. When you treat yourself to the movies or you finish a nice movie, thank yourself.

You've probably come across many online articles and read other books that tell you to tell yourself that you love yourself every day or to tell yourself that you're awesome in front of the mirror and well, I'm going to have to tell you the same thing. Practice self-affirmation. It's the most common piece of advice out there for loving yourself because it's one of the easiest and most effective.

Of course, just thanking yourself or telling yourself that you love yourself is not enough to make you learn to love yourself but it's one of the best things you can ever do for yourself. Remember how you're supposed to learn to love yourself? Doesn't loving a person include showing that you appreciate them? So why not appreciate yourself?

Just try to keep it internal, meaning don't just say it aloud in front of other people, at least not in the beginning. I'm telling you this because it could make you sound weird to other people. I remember my husband telling me about it when we had been dating for over a year. He told me how he used to think that it was weird how I kept saying "thank me" or "I love me" randomly - something I still do until now. It's become a habit for me now and it's something I tell my kids to practice although in a more private, internal manner.

Start your mornings with small words of appreciation. Tell yourself how awesome you are. Congratulate yourself for your achievements. Don't let your inner critic be the only one who gives you a negative opinion of you. Let your inner friend tell you how awesome you are too!

8. Evaluate Your Goals and Expectations and Adjust Accordingly

Have you heard of the saying that if you don't have any expectations, you'll never be disappointed? I'm going to recommend that you sort of do something similar. Frustration usually results when we can't seem to make something happen right? When you expect something to go your way but doesn't no matter how hard you try, you get frustrated. When you expect something good coming your way and you end up not getting it you get disappointed.

I'm not telling you to settle for the mediocre because that's like me telling you to just give up on yourself. What I'm trying to tell you is that maybe you should try to rethink your expectations of yourself. Maybe you've set some unrealistic goals for yourself that you will never reach and it's what's causing you to be frustrated and disappointed with yourself. It's complicated really. It's hard for me to explain this point without being self-contradictory so bear with me here.

Okay, let's start by doing a little self-evaluation. Remember how I said to work towards reaching your goals? Did I tell you to try to break down your goals into smaller, more manageable chunks right? What if no matter how little you break it down, the smaller pieces are still not something you can do? What do you do then?

A few years back I got to know someone whose job description is "Thermal Engineer." I have heard of civil engineers who work with construction, chemical engineers who work with chemicals, and mechanical engineers who work with cars but what does a thermal engineer do, work with heat? I was very curious about her job so I found myself asking her about her career. She gave me a long and detailed explanation which mostly flew over my head but from what I understood, she works for a company that makes satellites for commercial use, and she is in charge of making sure that a satellite they launch works once deployed despite going through the extreme temperatures that a satellite is subjected to from the heat of launching it through the atmosphere to the cold vacuum of space. Please don't take my word for it, like I said I don't think I understood it enough.

Anyway, it was a unique job that I haven't heard of before. It sounded awesome. When I asked her how and why she chose this job, she told me that her college degree is actually aeronautics engineering and that thermal engineer is just a title, again don't quote me on this. Apparently, her dream was to be an astronaut and while she is obviously smart enough to be working for NASA, becoming an astronaut means being one of the most physically fit humans to walk the earth and she wasn't fit enough to qualify.

I think she tried to apply but got rejected for the program or something like that and realizing that she would never qualify to become an astronaut, she decided to just work on rockets and other things that had to do with space. She realized that no matter how hard she tried, she would never achieve her dream simply because of the way her body was made and decided to settle for the next best thing. I'm sure you know people in your life who have worked really hard for their dreams but never achieved them so they ended up settling for something related instead. It's just how life is. Some things are simply out of reach no matter how hard you try. What do you do then? If life was a movie or a TV show and you're the main hero, you would keep trying and trying until through some stroke of luck or some extraordinary event you suddenly find yourself getting really close and grasping it but life isn't a movie.

Sometimes you just really have to give it up. Here's an approach that I think is appropriate. First, try to break down your goals into smaller, more achievable and realistic tasks. Try to judge if these tasks are something you can realistically achieve using your own abilities and if they are then go for it. If not, then try to ask yourself if you're okay with going for something that's related to it. Have you heard of the term S.M.A.R.T. goals? S.M.A.R.T. stands for Specific, Measurable, Attainable, Relevant and Time-Based. It's something my husband taught me once. He uses it to create his business plans and I think that it can be applied to personal goals as well.

Setting goals that way essentially means that you create goals that are well defined with measurable results that are within the scope of your abilities. You also have to take into consideration the different factors around you like your environment and social settings. Then, you should also create milestones that you work to reach within a certain period of time until you reach the end goal. If a goal is something that isn't S.M.A.R.T. then maybe you should consider setting a different goal or modify your goals to fit these criteria. Constantly getting frustrated and feeling disappointed is not going to help you find self-love so evaluate and adjust your goals and expectations accordingly.

9. Take Care of Yourself on The Outside Too

Have you given up on yourself? Do you go outside the house with your hair messed up, wearing dirty clothes and smelling like you haven't showered in days because you haven't? Do you think there's no point in making an effort? If you do then you need to change that right away. The way you look on the outside not only affects what others think of you but also affects the way you feel about yourself.

Do you know how salespeople and politicians have to look dignified to gain respect? You won't listen to a person selling you a car if they approach you looking like a homeless bum, would you? – Maybe if they're selling you drugs or some shady thing, then you would, but otherwise, you expect people to look the part right? A doctor wears a lab coat, a soldier wears a uniform, a salesman wears a suit. It's all to gain a certain air of respectability and credibility.

If you let yourself go around looking neglected then not only will other people lose respect for you, you will lose respect for yourself as well because you don't make an effort to look decent and respectable. While learning to control your thoughts and keep your emotions in check, don't forget to take care of your physical appearance too. Part of loving yourself is taking care of how you look. Exercise, eat healthily, make sure you're well-groomed and always wear nice, clean clothes.

10. Learn to Say No

Your friend's opinion might make them stop being your friend. You just agree to everything and go with whatever other people tell you to do because you think that saying no will make them dislike you. I understand, I was the same way once.

I found it hard to turn down people who asked me for favors because I was afraid that they'll hate me. I would bring extra sheets of paper so I would have enough to give to all the classmates who would ask. I would lend people my stuff and never ask for them back because I was afraid that they'll get angry with me. I lent people money and never collected because I was afraid of conflict. I always believed that it's better to just take the losses than to be at odds with other people.

I lost a lot of money and things because of this. I thought people respected me because they made the effort to be nice to me without realizing until later on that they were just being nice to me because they wanted to get something from me. I let myself believe that I was being nice and helpful and didn't realize until later that I wasn't being nice and helpful to myself. The people I was being nice to, the same people I thought I was helping out, all of them did not really respect me. To them, I was just someone who they can get things from.

It's interesting how it seems that the easier you are, the less people respect and value you. It's like supply and demand in economics. The less there is of something, the higher it's perceived value. Diamonds are rare so they command a high price tag while water is cheap because it's everywhere. The same applies to human social interaction. The worst part is, it's just not other people who lose respect for you but you also lose respect for yourself every time you go out of your way for people who don't even appreciate what you do for them.

Learn how to turn down people when they ask for something that's inconvenient for you. Learn the difference between giving because you want to and giving because you have to. The difference is how you feel about it. Giving because you want to feels good, while giving because you have to – because you're afraid of displeasing people is a burden that weighs you down.

11. Don't Let People Walk All Over You

Related to learning to say no, you also have to learn to stand up for yourself. You probably just let people walk over you because you're afraid of conflict. You always find yourself blindly agreeing to everything that other people say or do, even if it's something you're strongly opposed to because you're afraid that if you say something, they'll dislike you. You're afraid to complain or do anything even if your "friends" treat you unfairly because you believe that it's better than not having any friends at all.

In a way you're right. Not expressing your disagreement and just letting people walk all over you lets you avoid conflict but at the cost of your dignity. Each time you let something pass, your opinion of yourself just sinks lower. You try to please everybody because you're scared of people disliking you, but in doing so you end up disliking yourself.

Also when you're not expressing your discomfort or disagreement about something, you end up holding it in and that can only result in either you getting fed up one day and exploding violently or you end up turning against yourself which is what commonly happens.

Try practicing assertiveness, which is essentially knowing what you want and how to properly ask for it. You should never be afraid to let people know what you think and you should never be afraid of asking for what you want as long as you're doing it in a respectful and appropriate way. It also lets other people know that you're not someone they can just ignore or disrespect.

12. Forgive Yourself

In many cases, self-loathing is the product of guilt. You've done something that you can't forgive yourself for and you seem to not be able to forget about it either. Your inner critic keeps nagging you about it whenever a similar or related situation arises. For one reason or another, you can't let go and move on.

I've once come across a Vietnam war veteran who suffers from PTSD. He has done things during the war

Jennifer Butler Green

that he can't seem to forgive himself for. As a result, he became an abusive person who is always suspicious of other people's motives and did not know how to show his affection for his family.

While we can't really know for sure what goes on in his head, the fact that he had trouble trusting other people and show his affection gives us an insight of what goes on inside his head. He has trust issues because he is afraid that everyone is a potential threat. He is unable to properly express his love for his family because he is probably also unable to love himself.

If the reason for behind your self-loathing is that you have done something that you deeply regret, then the solution is to forgive yourself and let yourself move on. I know I make it sound easy, but forgiving yourself can sometimes be the hardest thing to do so I'm going to try to provide you with a few things that you can do to get into the path of forgiveness.

First, let's try to determine the thing or things you did that you can't forgive yourself for. If you paid attention in the first part of this book then you should have already been able to identify what these things are. What do you usually tell yourself when you recall these things? Do you tell yourself that there you could have done differently if only you knew something that you know now? If that's the case, then you have to know a few things. First, you can never take back the past. I know it hurts, but no matter what you do short of building and using a time machine, the past can never be changed.

Second and more importantly, there was no way you could have known back then. Maybe you should have known, but you didn't. You made the best decision based on the information you had at the time. Just as you can't go back to the past to fix it, there was also no way that you could have travelled to the future to know back then what you know now.

Third and most important of all, there was no way you could have known that it would turn out the way it did. I'm of course assuming that the result of what you did was not what you intended. That's why you regret it in the first place. The fact that you have regrets is good, it means you can tell right from wrong. The best thing you can do for yourself now is to learn from it and vow never to make the same mistake again.

In some cases, these regrets also come with its own set of limiting beliefs. You believe that you can never get over it. You believe that you're not good enough. You believe that you can never forgive yourself. It's time to challenge these beliefs. Give yourself more credit, you made it this far. Limiting thoughts and beliefs are part of our psychological and emotional defense mechanism. We limit ourselves because it's within the scope of what we know. Why don't you try exploring the unknown? Give yourself the benefit of a doubt and try moving past these limitations that you set for yourself.

Another thing you can do for yourself that would greatly help you move on is to repent. Repentance is something that you often hear in religious settings and what it means is not only to regret and ask for forgiveness but also to vow to be careful not to make the same mistake again, and to make reparations or to make up for the consequences of your mistake.

If you're guilty about hurting someone, then maybe you can ask for their forgiveness and help them out with something that they're struggling with. If it's not possible then you can instead help someone else. If you belong in any Christian denomination, you should at least be vaguely familiar with Saint Paul. He used to be named "Saul" and he was a big persecutor of the early Christians. He would either have them punished severely or killed. With the help of a miraculous vision, he became a Christian himself, changed his name to Paul and contributed greatly to the spread of Christianity in his time. The point I'm trying to make is that if simply forgiving yourself is not enough, then you can take it a step further and do something good to make up for whatever it is that you feel guilty about.

13. DO NOT Give Up on Yourself

This is very important. Do not ever give up on yourself. Learning to love yourself may not be easy after everything that you have been through and it's possible that you have tried and failed many times in the past to improve yourself, but nothing has ever worked out. Some things just take time and a lot of effort but do not ever give up on yourself.

Even if you feel like nobody would want to be friends with you, keep trying to approach and befriend people. Even if you feel ugly that nobody would want to pay attention to you, keep yourself clean and presentable. Even if you're afraid that people will dislike you if you refuse their requests, keep refusing them if you no longer feel like giving them anything.

If they stop being friends with you because you're no longer of any use to them, then they were never your friends in the first place, and you can always make new friends who will not use you.

As long as you're alive you can always improve yourself and your situation, you just have to keep trying and doing your best.

The Secret to Loving Yourself: The Long-Term Solution

Okay, so we're done with the quick fixes. Now that I look back, some of them aren't what most will consider quick or easy, but they're doable. I also promised to give you a major secret that many therapists use and it's time I delivered so here it is: *The best therapist you can ever get for yourself is none other than you.*

Was it disappointing? Believe it or not, I have just given you a really important piece of information. Before you throw away your e-reader or paperback in an open fire and curse my name, at least let me explain. I take what is called the Rogerian approach to Psychotherapy. It's an approach to psychotherapy that Carl Rogers, the man who developed the self-concept theory I mentioned earlier in this book developed. Here's what he said, in his own words: *It is the client who knows what hurts, what directions to go, what problems are crucial, what experiences have been deeply buried. It began to occur to me that unless I had a need to demonstrate*

"my own cleverness and learning, I would do better to rely upon the client for the direction of movement in the process." – Carl Rogers

Basically, he admits that nobody can truly ever know you better than you know yourself and unless we psychologists have a magic way to know you better than you know yourself, then the only one who can really ever get you to fully fix yourself is you. We practice what is called Client-Centered Therapy in which the therapist's goal is to simply act as a guide to let the client figure out how to fix himself or herself.

Now if you still feel upset about this, let me at least provide you with a guide on how this works. Rogers once identified a set of conditions that have to be met in order to be successful in client-based therapy and since I'm telling you to be your own therapist, you already cleared most of them. Now you just need one very important thing: Have unconditional positive regard for yourself.

Let me propose how you can do self-therapy. I want you to try a technique not very different from meditation. Here are the steps:

1. Find time to do this. Set a schedule, make it at least an hour a week but more is better. Now whatever you decide on, make sure to follow it.

2. Make sure you're in a comfortable environment with no distractions. Make sure your phone is on silent and make sure that nothing will distract you from this state. You can set an alarm or a timer to let you know that your session is over but until then, make sure that nothing will distract you unless there's an emergency.

3. Put yourself in a comfortable position. It doesn't have to be the Buddha pose or any specific thing. Just make sure you'll be comfortable with not moving from that position for the duration of your

session but at the same time don't get too comfortable that you'll just end up sleeping.

4. Close your eyes. Try to picture a specific room in your head. This room has to have a door that you can open and close behind you and that you can choose to enter or exit through this door at any time you wish. The room can be anything, but whatever it is it has to be a room where you can be comfortable talking. It has to be a room where everything said and done will not leave unless you give your explicit consent. It also has to be a room where you leave everything outside.

5. When you enter this room, your alarm or anyone from outside you can pull you back into reality but as much as possible when your alarm sounds or when someone or something from the real world distracts you or pulls you out, you will exit through the door.

6. Inside the room create a therapist. It has to be someone you're comfortable with. It can be a clone of you, it can be someone you look up to, it can be anyone as long as that person's only role is to

listen to you and that person is only inside that room and nowhere else and does not leave.

7. That therapist will listen to you unconditionally and will always be approving.

8. Talk to that therapist about anything and everything. All the things that bother you. All the things that hurt you. Your goals, your dreams, anything and everything that you want to talk about then together, come up with a plan of action on how you can love yourself.

9. At the end of each session, make sure to say goodbye and thank that therapist. Walk out the door, and close the door behind you.

10. Open your eyes and get back to reality. Do this as much as you need to.

11. That's it. At first, it's probably not going to be easy. Setting a schedule, taking this seriously, and creating a therapy simulation inside your head is probably going to take some time and practice to perfect but really, just take it seriously and keep at it. Eventually, you'll get really good at it that you can enter the therapy simulation anytime,

anywhere and you will be able to do it even without needing to set a schedule or being in a quiet room by yourself.

Now, I need you to really take this seriously if you want it to work. I know it doesn't sound easy and you might still be upset that I'm not giving you some specific advice or some big secret but you bought this book to learn to love yourself and fix what's wrong with you right? This is the big secret and this is the special advice. If you take it seriously, it's going to help get you closer to learning to love yourself and fix you from the inside.

VII. Conclusion

Having self-love is one of the best things to ever have for yourself. Learning to love yourself unconditionally is one of the greatest things you could ever do. Having self-love lets you feel complete on the inside, and in turn, this sense of completion will affect your personality and behavior and you will attract the right people and your life and make you see the world in a more positive light. People lose self-love in different ways according to different psychologists, but the common factor among all of their theories is that self-loathing is something you learned, not something you were born with.

In the first part of the book, we have tried to identify the different signs that let you recognize that you don't love yourself. It's when you don't care enough about yourself that you display behaviors that put yourself at risk, that keep you from realizing your own potential, and that makes you actively carry negative feelings about yourself.

We also discussed a few theories from known psychologists about how behavior and personality develop in people to better understand the different factors that cause a person to lose self-love. It's important to be able to identify the causes of self-loathing to create an understanding of the root of the problem. Understanding the source of the problem then leads to coming up with a better plan to solve the problem and that applies to self-love. The more you understand why you're having this problem, the better tools you can develop in order to fix the problem.

While the factors that contribute to this mostly start from childhood, it does not mean that they can't be fixed at any point after. Whatever you can learn can be unlearned and replaced with a new set of learning. It's not likely to be as easy but with determination and a consistent effort, you can learn to love yourself.

***

Are you happy with your life right now? What would make you happy? Do you have a plan for getting it? Would you like some help? I might be able to help you. Are you interested? Sign up for my newsletter. I give out a free workbook to help with social anxiety issues so those who sign up. I also give out limited copies of audiobook versions of my books. I also write more books and posting articles that can help deal with other issues related to social anxiety. There's a community that I'm building for people who are going through similar issues as you.

If it's okay with you, I'd also like to get your feedback so I can write more about things that could help you.

Does that sound like something that might interest you? I hope it does, because I need your help in helping others too. I have been in your shoes before, so I know how it feels. Join my newsletter and let's all help each other. Does that sound good? Visit my website now! The link is below and signup for my newsletter!

http://jen.green